Cover picture:
Boh Tea Plantations, Cameron Highlands, Malaysia 2012 D. Mangano

ISBN-10: 1481061402
ISBN-13: 978-1481061407

The Integrated Data Hub™

The Next Generation Data Warehouse

Dario Mangano

Dedication

To my wife Nathalie and my children, Eva and Theo.

To Mom and Dad.

You all believed in me.

Acknowledgements

First, thanks to my family for having the patience with me for having taken yet another challenge which decreases the amount of time I can spend with them. Specially Nathalie, my wife, who has taken a big part of that sacrifice, and also Eva and Theo, my children, who gave encouragements in their particular way. They and my parents, who forged my personality and share credit on every goal I achieve.

Thanks to all my present and former team members for sharing my happiness when starting this project and following with encouragement when it seemed too difficult to be completed. I would have probably given up without their support and example on what to do when you really want something.

Speaking of encouragement, I must mention that Hans Hultgren is responsible for having me wrote this book: first by mentoring me on Data Vault and later by insisting that I should share part of what I have learned on this book. He is a great person and I can only be grateful to have met him.

And thanks to M. Jean-Marc Tassin, my first employer, who gave me the chance to have a really good start in my professional life.

Special thanks to Selma, Cedric, Jean, Ramzi and Yan for their daily support.

I do not forget of course my reviewer's team: Hans, Ramzi, Cedric, Jean-François and Joelle.

Foreword by Hans Hultgren

Data Warehouse projects fail. As an industry we have been battling with this phenomenon for decades. Though we have been getting better over the years, as an industry we still have a long way to go.

Fortunately some people have found ways to beat the odds. By thinking out of the box, formulating new ideas, and creating new innovative approaches these people have each somehow unlocked the secrets of successful DW programs.

Within this group there are those who have fire tested their theories with real life deployments. They have proven the merits of their ideas with perhaps the only test that really matters – actually deploying successful DW programs.

Now this is a small group, a special club, and of the few members in this club, an even smaller group is willing and able to communicate and share their ideas.

In this book, Integrated Data Hub™, Dario Mangano shares with us his ideas including the solution he developed and the proven architecture that he has successfully deployed in several organizations.

This book is a guide to a successful data warehousing business intelligence (DWBI) program.

One of the success factors is recognizing that there is no success to be found in a data warehouse *project*. To leverage enterprise data we have to recognize two things; first that the data warehouse is not a project with a beginning and end but rather an ongoing program, and second that this program is not technically driven but actually business and information driven.

The Integrated Data Hub™ is an organizational information framework that takes into account the dynamic characteristics of the data warehouse function. Business alignment, data integration and historization are ongoing dynamic functions that need to respond to changes in the business, changes in the sources, and changes in downstream requirements.

The organizational need for enterprise-wide data is an increasingly important component of enterprise management. With this increasing importance comes also an increasing need for traceability and auditability. Dario explains how the role of the business intelligence department is to manage the transformation of integrated and trusted data into understandable information with real business meaning.

Dario's IDH leverages the concepts and principles of both Bill Inmon's data warehouse and corporate information factory, and of Ralph Kimball's dimensional modeling and data marts. Insofar as the goals of the IDH require an optimized modeling paradigm, Dario has specified the use of the data vault modeling approach.

Dario starts by sketching the historical background and then introduces the IDH concept. Keep reading as Dario weaves the IDH components together into an effective strategy and a cohesive blueprint for enterprise information management. From a modeling perspective this book takes us from 3NF and Star Schemas to Data Vault and Dario's own Leaf Schemas. From an architectural perspective this book describes the component layers and their specific characteristics.

This book is a great addition to the IP for the new age of data warehousing and information management.

Data Warehouse programs using the IDH™ succeed. And perhaps that is the most compelling reason to read this book. Thank you Dario for sharing your framework with us!

Hans Patrik Hultgren.

Hans is an author, advisor, speaker and industry analyst in the data warehousing and business intelligence industry. He is the President of Genesee Academy LLC, a global provider of training seminars and certifications and also a provider of DWBI e-Learning through DataVaultAcademy.com. Follow on Twitter: gohansgo Blog: HansHultgren.wordpress.com

Hans is the author of the recently published book Modeling the Agile Data Warehouse with Data Vault which is available on Amazon websites.

Table of Contents

Section I

Where we speak about Data Warehousing

CHAPTER 1
Introduction

1.1 A Fast Moving World

Already more than 22 years since I started my professional career, and Data Management is taking every day a greater place in my life.

I must admit that it is somehow normal, since I specialized myself in Business Intelligence!

At that time, I was far from imagining that the data would play an increasingly more important role in enterprise management.

Indeed, any modern company willing to stay competitive, must pay particular attention to the data stored in its operational databases and especially they have to put in place strategies to transform these data into valuable information allowing the executives to take quickly smarter decisions.

The data coming from outside the company, as well as those you can buy or rent to perform direct marketing campaigns for example or collected from social networks, so called big data, must also be integrated to the enterprise data used by modern companies' executives to take their decisions.

World trade globalization and the increasing speed of the trade exchanges, lead towards more and more reconciliations between formerly competing firms. The phenomenon of mergers and acquisitions is also increasing rapidly and as a result the integration of data coming from systems which were not designed to work together is a challenge not to be under estimated. Numerous mergers of international companies have failed due to their inability to integrate their databases.

Mergers and acquisitions (*abbreviated* **M&A**) *is an aspect of corporate strategy, corporate finance and management dealing with the buying, selling, dividing and combining of different companies and similar* entities *that can help an enterprise grow rapidly in its sector or location of origin, or a new field or new location, without creating a subsidiary, other child entity or using a joint venture. The distinction between a "merger" and an "acquisition" has become increasingly blurred in various respects (particularly in terms of the ultimate economic outcome), although it has not completely disappeared in all situations.*

(From Wikipedia, the free encyclopedia)

When these M&A occur, but also during the normal life of a modern company, it is not uncommon to see the information systems of these companies modified or replaced. The new one co-existing with elder for sometimes a very long period. Eventually, some geographical subsidiaries of these companies will continue with their previous systems, while the headquarters and the more mature subsidiaries will already be migrated to the new one.

These periods of coexistence of heterogeneous IT ecosystems can last for a long time. As a consequence Information Managers have to deploy data integration strategies to continue to provide the same level of services, with the right level of accuracy of the data transmitted to the executives. These strategies must allow them to take their decisions based on validated data and to lead their companies in these critical periods.

As an example, think about the M&A that occurred during the last 15 years in the sector of airlines companies, telecommunication companies or major banks.

The Bank Of America group is a good example to illustrate the challenges that their IT executives had to face during the last two decades.

Since 1990, the Bank Of America's information systems had to integrate data coming from the banks that they bought as NationsBank, FleetBoston Financial, MBNA

America Bank, Banco Itau, The United States Trust Company, LaSalle Bank Corporation and Merrill Lynch to name only the most important.

As of 2010, **Bank of America** *is the fifth-largest company in the United States by total revenue, as well as the third-largest non-oil company in the U.S. (after Walmart and General Electric). In 2010, Forbes listed* **Bank of America** *as the 3rd biggest company in the world.*

(From Wikipedia, the free encyclopedia)

Customers of these companies, in fact you and me, are very concerned about the protection of their personal data and at the same time appreciate being addressed with customized tailored messages and personalized offerings. They quickly reject companies that send repeatedly conflicting messages.

The inability for a company to correctly and quickly integrate all these data sources, often lead them to send incorrect messages to their customers resulting in a loss of revenue and credibility that might prove to be fatal.

1.2 New Challenges

Regularly confronted with such challenges, I started to work on the concept of an enterprise data warehouse, to ensure my managers an optimal quality of their data as well as a single version of the truth across the whole company.

This notion of a single version of the truth is vital for many decision makers. To make decisions based on the data provided to them, these executives need to have a total confidence in the way these data are produced.

In addition these data must be transformed into understandable information with a real business meaning. The role of the Business Intelligence department is to manage these transformations.

The object of this book is to provide a Corporate Data Warehouse architecture, not only to ensure the quality of the data and to allow the production of one single version of the truth across the entire enterprise, but also a way to absorb at lower cost, the numerous changes that will undoubtedly occur to the source systems.

I have been working on this architecture for more than a decade now and I have had the opportunity to deploy it in several multinational groups confronted with important changes of their application landscape.

I call this architecture The Integrated Data Hub™, and for me this is not only the next generation Data Warehouse but also "the smartest way to deal with your data integration challenges"

Data integration *involves combining data residing in different sources and providing users with a unified view of these data. This process becomes significant in a variety of situations, which include both commercial (when two similar companies need to merge their databases) and scientific (combining research results from different bioinformatics repositories, for example) domains. Data integration appears with increasing frequency as the volume and the need to share existing data explodes. It has become the focus of extensive theoretical work, and numerous open problems remain unsolved. In management circles, people frequently refer to data integration as "Enterprise Information Integration" (EII).*

(From Wikipedia, the free encyclopedia)

In this book I will describe, one by one, all the components of the Integrated Data Hub™, as well as the best practices to put in place in order to make its implementation a success and achieve its objectives.

CHAPTER 2
From Data, To Information, To Knowledge

2.1 Raw data are not enough

As discussed in the previous chapter, in order to allow executives to take smart and quick decisions, the Information Manager must provide them with accurate data.

Most of the time, raw data is not sufficient to take a decision. These data must be transformed into relevant information.

The role of a Business Intelligence department is to put in place strategies and tools to transform these data into information.

But, what is exactly the difference between data and information? People often miss the subtle difference between data and information and use the words interchangeably.

Data are raw, unorganized facts that need to be processed. Data can be something simple and seemingly random and useless until it is organized.

When data are processed, organized, structured or presented in a given context so as to make it useful, it is called Information.

As an example, in a given college, each student's test score is one piece of data. The class' average score or the college's average score is the information that can be concluded from the given data.

It is not enough to have data. Data in themselves are fairly useless. But when these data are interpreted and processed to determine its true meaning, they become useful and can be called Information. Data is the computer's language. Information is our translation of this language.

2.2 Information is necessary

Timely and useful information requires accurate data. To achieve accurate information, the data must be stored and generated properly. Also, the data must be stored in a format that is easy to access and process. And like any basic resource, the data environment must be managed carefully. Thus, Data Management is a discipline that focuses on the proper generation, storage, and retrieval of data.

> ➤ *Data constitute the building blocks of information.*
>
> ➤ *Information is produced by processing data.*
>
> ➤ *Information is used to reveal the meaning of data.*
>
> ➤ *Good, relevant, and timely information is the key to good decision making.*

Now that we agreed that data are not enough to enable decision making, and that we have to transform these data into meaningful information, it is time to ask ourselves if these newly generated information, is enough or if we can go a step ahead and continue these transformations to even better help the executives to take better and quicker decision!

A step ahead?

Yes, it is possible. We can transform this information into knowledge!

2.3 Knowledge is better

Most of the people agree that knowledge and information are two distinct concepts. But do they also agree upon the differences that separate the two concepts? Not really.

In my opinion information refers to general data expressed by numbers, words, images, sounds and so on. Bear in mind that these data can be elaborated or not. The observed outcome of a scientific experiment, for example, is data that has not being elaborated. A report explaining the findings of such experiment, on the other hand, is elaborated data.

Knowledge refers to the practical use of information. While information can be transported, stored or shared without many difficulties the same cannot be said about knowledge. Knowledge necessarily involves a personal experience. Referring back to the scientific experiment, a third person reading the results will have information about it, while the person who conducted the experiment personally will have knowledge about it.

Another view of this difference could be synthesized by this simple sentence: Information is knowledge only if it is shared!

It is very important to have this difference clear, especially in our internet-based society. Today information is freely available to anyone anywhere in the world. An eighteen year old boy from India could easily search on the web and find all the information ever produced about a tonsillectomy. But I am not sure whether I would like to have this same boy performing that surgery on myself... what about you?

> ➢ *Data will only have a meaningful use if we are able to get vital or key information out of it in such a way that it can generate useful applications that we needed.*
>
> ➢ *This information will only be more useful when you are able to understand, rationalize, communicate, relate, apply, and share it to others. That way, others will have a common understanding or rationalization as you and most probably, can also generate more information that can grow exponentially. In a much shorter explanation, these information can be proven useful if synthesized by more than one head to make it more holistic.*
>
> ➢ *This information where acquisition involves complex cognitive processes: perception, learning, communication, association and reasoning eventually transformed into knowledge that can rationalize into much more diverse and greater concepts or applications.*

As this knowledge is growing exponentially, it now requires management, making the most out of this knowledge generated. This is Knowledge Management.

2.4 The DIKW Model

In a nutshell, Knowledge Management focuses on a higher level of getting the desired objectives i.e. performance improvement, competitive advantage, innovation, sharing of best practices, continuous improvement, etc.

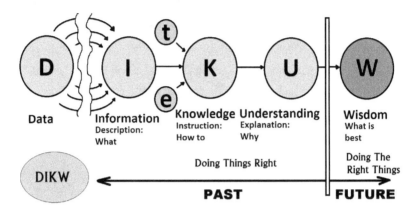

Figure 1: The DIKW Model

*A flow diagram of the DIKW hierarchy; where d : data, i :
information, k : knowledge, u : understanding, w : wisdom, t : tacit
knowledge, and e : explicit knowledge*

The relationship between Data, Information and Knowledge is often referred as the DIK pyramid. A few years ago some authors added the concept of Wisdom, making the DIKW model a new standard.

The DIKW Pyramid, *also known variously as "DIKW Hierarchy", "Wisdom Hierarchy", "Knowledge Hierarchy", "Information Hierarchy", and "Knowledge Pyramid", refers loosely to a class of models for representing purported structural and/ or functional relationships between data, information, knowledge, and wisdom. "Typically information is defined in terms of data, knowledge in terms of information, and wisdom in terms of knowledge".*

Not all versions of the DIKW model reference all four components (earlier versions not including data, later versions omitting or downplaying wisdom), and some include additional components. In addition to a hierarchy and a pyramid, the DIKW model has also been characterized as a chain, as a framework and as a continuum.

(From Wikipedia, the free encyclopedia)

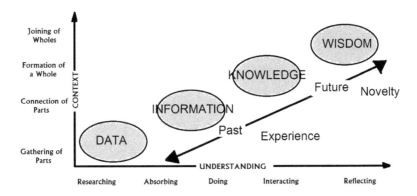

Figure 2: The DIKW Graph

It is now clear, that transforming data into information is a mandatory but not sufficient step in our effort to help executives to take their decisions. We have to make this information available to people who enrich it with their own experience and understanding. In a word, we have to enable the transformation of this information into knowledge.

Based on this knowledge, we will enable actions.

This sentence could be the motto of any Business Intelligence department: "From Data, To Information, To Knowledge, To Actions!"

In fact, I have made this sentence my personal motto for a very long time now.

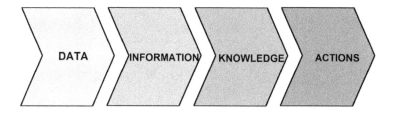

Figure 3: The DIKA Model

In order to perform all these transformations, to provide the executives with a single point of access for validated information, to absorb with a minimum of impact all the changes of the data sources, we have to choose the most adapted architecture.

The detailed architecture of the Integrated Data Hub™ will be described later, but in order to explain why I believe traditional Data Warehouse models are no more adapted to face the huge challenges modern companies will face in the coming years, I have to spend some time talking about the history of Data Warehousing, starting by the very beginning: The Operational Data Store (ODS).

CHAPTER 3
The Operational Data Store

3.1 At the beginning was the ODS

At the beginning was the Operational Data Store!

Every book dealing with Data Warehousing or Data Integration could begin with this simple sentence!

Indeed, since the very beginning of IT, users wanted to make lists and reports with the data generated by the enterprise.

IT people's early jobs was to extract data and to present it to deciders. But soon, it appeared that large queries against operational systems strongly decreased their performances.

Early Data Managers decided that it was cleverer to design a dedicated database in order to run these heavy queries and generate the requested reports.

These specialized databases populated by a replication of the production data and exclusively destined to generated lists and reports were called operational Data Store (ODS).

In these early days, it was obvious that the best approach was to replicate the design of the source systems. The first ODS were thus made of a collection of VSAM files, some years later it was mainly composed of hierarchical tables, and since the last 20 years, Third Normal Form relational Data Bases is the norm..

Soon, ODS were adapted to do some Data Integration and validation of very simple business rules and to keep a certain level of historization of the source data.

Remember, these ODS were first designed to allow operational reporting and to relieve operational systems from the weight of large queries running against them.

---

*An **Operational Data Store** (or "ODS") is a database designed to integrate data from multiple sources for additional operations on the data. The data is then passed back to operational systems for further operations and to the data warehouse for reporting.*

Because the data originates from multiple sources, the integration often involves cleaning, resolving redundancy and checking against business rules for integrity. An ODS is usually designed to contain low-level or atomic (indivisible) data (such as transactions and prices) with limited history that is captured "real time" or "near real time" as opposed to the much greater volumes of data stored in the data warehouse generally on a less-frequent basis.

(From Wikipedia, the free encyclopedia)

With the advent, a few years later, of the Data Warehouse, the ODS were destined to disappear, and yet, they still exists in numerous modern enterprise's data architectures. Why?

Simply because they are probably the best source to feed the Data Warehouse and they host validated and integrated data, but also because this is the only place in the enterprise where you can find data that does not exist anymore in the source systems and a historization of all the changes applied to the data.

So, if the ODS is so essential, why do Data Managers decide a few years later to build additional data bases like Data Warehouses and Data Marts ?

Because we entered the era of the Key Performance Indicators!

3.2 The growing Importance of KPIs

KPI lists are the new bible of top executives. They never start their working day without taking a look to their KPIs. The KPIs tells everything about the health of a company. And in order to provide the right KPI, at the right time to the right audience, you have to transform data into information!

Sound familiar?

To transform data into Key Performance Indicators, some business rules, including complex aggregations and statistics must be performed.

As the ODS is tailored for operational reporting, data architects decided to perform these transformations in another dedicated database.

This dedicated architecture is commonly called the Data Warehouse

3.3 And Then The Data Warehouse

Considered by many to be the Father of Data Warehousing, Bill Inmon first began to discuss the principles around the Data Warehouse and even coined the term in the 1970s. In 2007, Inmon was named by Computerworld as one of the "Ten IT People Who Mattered in the Last 40 Years."

Throughout the latter 1970s into the 1980s, Inmon worked extensively as a data professional, honing his expertise in all manners of relational Data Modeling. Inmon's work as a Data Warehousing pioneer took off in the early 1990s when he ventured out on his own, forming his first company, Prism Solutions. One of Prism's main products was the Prism Warehouse Manager, one of the first industry tools for creating and managing a Data Warehouse.

In 1992, Inmon published Building the Data Warehouse, one of the seminal volumes of the industry. Currently in its fourth edition, the book continues to be an important part of any data professional's library with a fine-tuned mix of theoretical background and real-world examples.

We have seen earlier that decision makers and analysts needed validated KPIs to lead their companies and to take smarter decisions. But, what do they do with these KPIs?

If you take a closer look to the reports used by these executives, you will probably see that they always cross these KPIs with other indicators, they perform time series calculations, they try to draw trends by comparing historical data with current data, etc.

In a word, they do what we call Business Intelligence!

3.4 Business Intelligence

Analysts are always crossing dimensions to measure facts.

This sentence seems complex, but in reality it is very simple and it is the base of modern Business Intelligence.

Imagine a manager of a car company. He wants to know the number of cars sold by his company. The number of car sold is a fact, or a measure. He wants to know the number of cars sold by type and by year, it means that he will perform a dimensional analysis, and that he will cross two dimensions to obtain a fact. Here the two dimensions are the Product one, and the Time one.

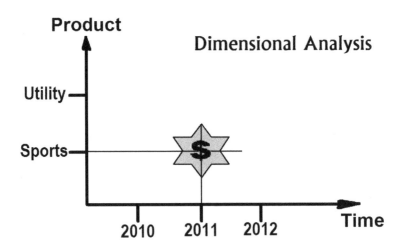

Figure 4: Dimensional Analysis

Obviously, the ODS, that is built to perform operational reporting, is not the right place to perform this kind of query: Indeed the structure itself of the ODS, that is the as similar as possible to the structure of the source system, is not designed to be performant to manage aggregates data nor complex time series queries comparisons.

3.5 Dimensional Analysis

Ralph Kimball, the other father of Data Warehousing proposed in the late 90s, an architecture dedicated and specialized to manage queries destined to perform dimensional analysis.

The two architectures are very often opposed, but I personally believe that the truth lies somewhere in the middle! Both approaches have their pros and cons; this is what I will present in the next chapter.

CHAPTER 4
The Data Warehouse: Inmon's and Kimball's Views

4.1 The Data Warehouse Schism

In 1992, Bill Inmon published Building the Data Warehouse, one of the most important books in the Data Management field. Even today, the 4th edition of this important publication, continues to be a must have in any data professional's library.

At the end of the 1990s Inmon developed his concept of Corporate Information Factory. The CIF is actually a corporate view of the data, and the Enterprise Data Warehouse is only one part of the CIF Concept. This enterprise level view of the data is something the IDH™ concept share with Inmon's CIF concept.

Third Normal Form modeling is still at the heart of Inmon's approach to Data Warehouse design. His main idea here is to guarantee an enterprise-wide consistency by sticking as close as possible to the design of the sources systems. This approach differs fundamentally from the "other" father of Data Warehousing, Ralph Kimball and both differ from the one I develop in the IDH™ concept.

> ***Bill Inmon*** *created the accepted definition of what a data warehouse is - a subject oriented, nonvolatile, integrated, time variant collection of data in support of management's decisions. Compared with the approach of the other pioneering architect of data warehousing, Ralph Kimball, Inmon's approach is often characterized as a top-down approach.*
>
> (From Wikipedia, the free encyclopedia)

At the beginning of the 21st Century, a schism grew between the differing architectural philosophies of Inmon and Kimball. But it is important to mention here that Bill Inmon wrote the foreword for The Data Warehouse Toolkit, the 1st Kimball's book. He called Kimball's work "…one of the definitive books of our industry. If you take the time to read only one professional book, make it this book."

As mentioned earlier, Inmon proposes a top down philosophy by championing a large centralized Data Warehouse approach.

On the other hand, Kimball proposes a "bottom up" approach favoring the development of individual data marts at the departmental level that get integrated together using the Information Bus architecture.

I personally prefer to integrate these two seminal concepts and to take the best of both approaches, adding some additional functionalities and practices in order to better cope with the modern challenges of data integration.

4.2 The New Data Warehousing's Challenges

The data industry is living a complete revolution. This revolution will of course affect Data Warehousing. Real-time data analysis and Cloud storage will obviously play an important role in the practice's evolution.

The presentation layer, read the end-user side, will also rapidly evolve by making mobile and web access a standard by default. Note to mention, the growing impact of the collaborative Business Intelligence.

The ability to manage unstructured data will also become a mandatory requirement in any future EDW implementation.

The widely used term "Big Data" obviously also plays its role in today's modern Data Warehousing practice.

> ***Big data*** *in general is defined as high volume, velocity and variety information assets that demand cost-effective, innovative forms of information processing for enhanced insight and decision making.*
>
> (Gartner)

With the emerging of rules like the Sarbanes-Oxley Act, data quality and governance will grow in relevance concerning the management of Data Warehouses.

And finally, whether you opt for the top-down or bottom-up approach or a mixture of the two, integrating a warehouse with the organization's overall Data Architecture remains a key principle.

As the Data Warehousing practice enters the third decade in its history, Bill Inmon and Ralph Kimball still play active and relevant roles in the industry. Their fundamental work in the 80s and early 90s largely defined a sector of the data profession that continues to evolve today.

I personally believe, and I know that Bill Inmon does as well, that it is time to reconcile the two approaches and to integrate new architectural components in order to answer the coming challenges.

This is what I call the Unified view of Data Warehousing. And this unified view must be based on a solid architecture, but also on a collection of best practices. All this can be found inside The Integrated Data Hub™.

Section II

Where we speak about Reunification

CHAPTER 5
The Data Warehouse: A Unified View

5.1 The Truth Lies Somewhere In The Middle

Nowadays, in most companies, Information Architects implement a hybrid approach, combining the best of both worlds, using an Operational Data Store as a source for a Kimball like Dimensional Bus.

---

*A **Bus Architecture** is composed of a set of tightly integrated data marts that get their power from conformed dimensions and fact tables.*

*A **Conformed Dimension** is defined and implemented one time, so that it means the same thing everywhere it's used. Fact tables that should be conformed include those that derive revenue, profit, standard prices, and standard costs.*

The advantage of the dimensional bus architecture is the implementation of the concept of conformed dimensions.

(Michelle A. Poolet, 2007)

The data integration and the application of corporate business rules, are partly done in the ODS, and in the Data Marts.

In my opinion, this solution is not sustainable for at least two reasons.

Firstly, I see an important problem of historization of the business rules that are applied to the data.

Some authors interpret the Inmon's definition of Data Warehousing, and claim that an Enterprise Data Warehouse should be rebuilt from scratch on demand.

If you stick to this fundamental rule, it means that you have to find an architecture able to store the historization of the business rules.

As an example, imagine that you have to reload your enterprise Data Warehouse from scratch, and want to calculate an indicator like the average consumption of a product, and that the definition of the Corporate Business Rule defined to calculate this KPI varied over time.

With the Inmon or the Kimball approaches or even with a hybrid approach you will have to violate important basic of each of these seminal philosophies.

Obviously, the solution could be to build an intermediate layer, to do this kind of historization.

The second inconvenience of the Dimensional Bus Architecture, is the historization of some attributes of a conformed dimension.

A dimension able to track historization is called Slowly Changing Dimension.

*Dimensions that change over time are called **Slowly Changing Dimensions**. For instance, a product price changes over time; People change their names for some reason; Country and State names may change over time. These are a few examples of Slowly Changing Dimensions since some changes are happening to them over a period of time.*

Slowly Changing Dimensions are often categorized into three types namely Type1, Type2 and Type3.

With slowly changing dimensions you can respond in one of three ways.

- You can overwrite the old data with the new data, which works best when the old data has no significance and can be discarded.

- You can create a new dimension record for the time period that defines the change, which works best with changes that neatly partition history.

- You can also create an "old value" column in the slowly changing

dimension to store the previous value, which works best with soft changes.

(Michelle A. Poolet, 2007)

If you want to apply a Slowly Changing Dimension Historization Type II, on one attribute of a huge dimension, the Kimball's rule implies to create a new record of the whole dimension.

Even if Kimball calls it Slowly Changing Dimension, we all agree that these changes in important attributes can occur very frequently, especially since the users required near real time loading of the data.

5.2 A New Approach to deal with New Challenges.

In addition to these two major inconvenient of the traditional approach of data warehousing, I see a lot of small issues to be solved during the implementation of an Enterprise Data Warehouse.

After several years of tempting to solve these issues by implementing hybrid architecture, difficult to maintain and not corresponding to any described, documented and accepted by enterprise architects definition, I finally decided to create my own approach.

With this approach, that I call The Integrated Data Hub™, I try to solve the issues listed above, and to create a scalable architecture in order to deal with modern Data Integration challenges, to continue to respect the basic rules published by the fathers of Data Warehousing, and to bring my own experience on this matter.

I will talk about concepts like, Parallelism, Restartability, Master Data Management, Business Rules Engine, Rejection and Recycling Strategies, Data Lineage, Impact Analysis, Orchestration, Logical Unit Of Work, Meta Driven Automation, Generic Data Model, Ensemble Modeling, Bi-directional Hub of Data, Canonization of data, Message Oriented Change Data Capture, to mention only the most important.

CHAPTER 6
The Integrated Data Hub™

6.1 The Integrated Data Hub™ Defined

The Integrated Data Hub™ is a Hub of Integrated Data.

A Hub because, it is the place where all the data of the enterprise, that has to be validated by corporate business rules, will have to go through.

A Hub because the IDH™ communicates with the surrounding environment in every direction. West with the source systems, North with the Service layer, East with the target system, (mainly Business Intelligence but also other operational systems) and South with the Metadata layer.

Integrated, because, the main purpose of the IDH™ is to give the user a single version of the truth. You will thus find all data related to a business concept in a single place.

We could add to the concept of Integrated Data, those of Non Volatile, Time Variant and Subject Oriented, to stick with the Inmon's definition of the Enterprise Data Warehouse.

The Integrated Data Hub™ is a reference architecture for Data Integration but it is also a set of concepts, a development framework, a set of best practices and includes other technical considerations.

This Data Integration Reference Architecture is based on different layers, each one having its own and only purpose.

In addition to architectural considerations, you will find behind the IDH™ concept a set of guidelines and best practices to ensure that this architecture is built to answer the future challenges of Data Integration.

This architecture was thought to be most relevant when:

- Your EDWH has to be fault resistant
- Your EDWH is supposed not to be impacted by changes in the surrounding environment, and particularly when new sources are added frequently or existing ones change often.
- Business rules are subject to change over time.
- Auditability is required.
- The structure of arriving data is not always known.
- Historization and time slices are required.

6.2 A Layered Architecture

As described before, The Integrated Data Hub™ is at first a Data Integration reference layered architecture.

Each layer will be described in details in the next chapters, but I will start listing them here:

- The Staging Layer

    You will find here mainly a copy the source systems tables and a delta load of the data needed to refresh the EDW. Small transformations can occur in a second phase of the staging layer.

- The HiST Layer

    Here you will find a complete historization of the staging layer, in order to provide a valid source to reload the data warehouse and to perform operational reporting.

- The Core Data Warehouse Layer

    This is where the data integration and the decoupling with the source systems are achieved. The Data Model is mainly business oriented. Historization and data lineage are performed here also.

- The Presentation Layer

This is where you will find the data marts designed to answer business questions and to do Analytical Reporting, but also all the needed structures to perform your Consolidated Operational Reporting

- The Access Layer

    Mainly composed of a corporate semantic layer.

- The Metadata Layer

    This is where we record every action done on and with the data going through the IDH™. The main purpose of this layer is to allow full data lineage and impact analysis.

- The Service Layer

    This is one of the main concepts behind the IDH™. You will find the MDM engine, The Business Rules Engine, the Orchestration services, etc.

- The Message Oriented Layer

    Another important concept of the

IDH™. The ability of the Data Hub to communicate in all directions using canonical data embedded into messages.

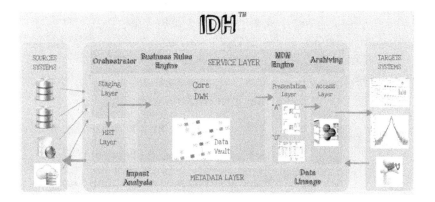

Figure 5 - A Layered Architecture

6.3 Other IDH™ Concepts

As mentioned before, The IDH™ is not only a data integration reference architecture, but it is also a set of guidelines and best practices.

The concepts will also be developed in the next chapters, but let me first list it here:

- The Logical Unit Of Work

    This is the biggest part of code that is allowed to be written by an ETL developer. It must be designed keeping three main concepts in mind: Restartability, Parallelism, and

Orchestration. A Logical Unit Of Work is supposed to do only data movement from one border of a layer, to the other border of the following layer. All other parasites work has to be performed by a service.

- Meta Data Driven Automation

    This concept would allow avoiding the use of traditional ETL engine. The idea here is to describe the transformations you want to see applied to the data, and the orchestrator service will do the rest.

- Rejection and Recycling

    This is one of the major components of the service layer. It must allow to reject data based on rules, and to recycle them during the next load of the EDW.

- Business Ownership and Natural Language

    Another important concept is the fact that all business rules are described in a natural language by the owner of the business rule, normally the business. These business rules must be historized in order to reload the EDW with a correct picture of the past. The Metadata Driven Automation service will manage the application of these business rules.

CHAPTER 7
The Staging Layer

7.1 Staging, Staging, Staging!

I attended my first Data Warehouse training more than fifteen (15) years ago! And I was taught at that time, that the more you stage the data during data movement, the better it is.

So many years later, despite all the technology advances and "in memory" capabilities, I still believe in this early learning.

---

*To **stage the data** means that we store the data.*

*If we **persist the data** it means that we store, maintain and keep these data in a database for the life of these data.*

It is why, in the IDH™ reference architecture, you will find so many layers, and in my opinion, a layer should be physically stored in your database.

And, as in any Datawarehouse architecture, in the IDH™, you will find a first layer called the Staging Area or Staging Layer.

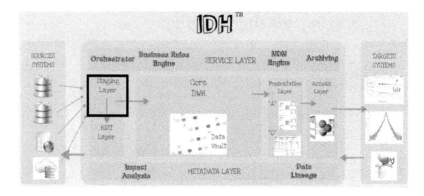

Figure 6 - The Staging Layer

The staging layer stores raw data extracted from each of the disparate source data systems.

> The main purpose of the **Staging Layer** (or the processing from source to staging) is to load source data into the Data Warehouse environment for further processing. In other words, the Staging Layer is responsible for the physical movement of data from the source platform onto the Data Warehouse platform. However, there are already some concepts built in this layer that are foundational to the rest of the system. Examples are the definition of the correct event datetime, delta selection and streamlining of the data types. No alterations / transformations to the data contents or its structure will be done.
>
> (Ravo's Business Intelligence)

The design of a reliable and scalable data hub is outlined

and carried out by functional and non-functional requirements. Examples of some of these requirements include items such as the following:

- The amount of raw source data to retain after it has been processed through the ETL data lifecycle.

- The acceptable levels of data quality, related baselines and metrics as stated by the Data Governance Board.

- The masking/scrambling of sensitive data within staging areas

- The identification of recoverable artifacts in the event of disasters, etc.

With these types of requirements, rules and decisions, a scalable and secured framework is firmly in place to facilitate the defined ETL methodology. These data sources go through a number of evolutionary stages in order to build a robust and comprehensive data warehouse. Moreover, as great data architects that we are, we know that these stages must include the following:

7.2 Data Acquisition

This activity comprises landing the data physically or

logically in order to initiate the ETL processing lifecycle. The staging area here could include a series of sequential files, relational or federated data objects. Nevertheless, the design of intake area or landing zone must enable the subsequent ETL processes, as well as provide direct links and/or integrating points to the metadata repository so that appropriate entries can be made in that repository for all data sources landing in the intake area.

7.3 Data Profiling

Data profiling is the inspection of the source data panorama to obtain an understanding of the condition of the data sources. In most profiling attempts, this means generating various reports with any number of metrics, statistics, and counts that reflect the quality of the source data coming in.

7.4 Data Cleansing

Data cleansing is an iterative set of operations that starts and ends with the business rules and standards around acceptable data quality levels from the Data Governance Board (e.g. 95% of the data meets the quality standards). This comprehends explorative work to provide additional detail in detecting data patterns and design options for quality enforcement at the attribute, record and aggregate levels and data correction jobs to fill in missing or incomplete data and correct data values. There is also the analysis of reports based on the findings and results of the investigation and data correction jobs to determine if further clarifications and/or modifications are to be made.

Notice that depending of the structure and the model of your next layer, in the case of the IDH™ the Core Data Warehouse Layer, you could choose not to clean the data, and to store the data as they are in the DWH.

This last approach is the one I choose for my IDH™ reference architecture mainly because I am convinced that the best Modeling Technique for the EDW is Data Vault. But I will extensively explain this in another chapter.

7.5 Data Standardization and Matching

Data standardization and matching is a set of processes that essentially consists of the design and execution of standardizing jobs to create uniformity around specific compulsory data elements. This comprises the design and execution of matching and de-duplicating jobs to eliminate duplicate data and create a single version of the truth. It also includes the analysis of reports related to errors and/or exceptions and determines if further clarifications or modifications are to be made (if required) and to assess the readiness for data delivery to the data warehouse and ODS.

7.6 Data Transformation

Transforming data basically means converting data to conform to a standard established by the Data Governance Board. Examples of data transformations comprise converting nulls to specific values, gender codes that are disparate to a common set of values or even merging multiple source fields to one data element.

Here also, you can choose to store the data in the EDW as they arrive without any transformation not formatting and choose a generic data format in order to make your architecture more fault resistant.

Because of my personal choice for the Data Vault design methodology; this last approach is the one I will choose for the IDH™.

7.7 Data Loading

Depending on business requirements, the loading phase can comprise a total data refresh of the target component or adding new data to the data component in a historical manner. Loading to a staged copy of the target component empowers a series of validation exercises. This includes verification of referential integrity, data quality and transformation rules prior to the actual data population of the Enterprise Data Warehouse and/or ODS.

7.8 Design and Construction

The creation of a staging area will generally start with the typical exercise of the design of any data environment. Tasks such as server configuration, alignment of file systems, creating the database instances and related database objects are common elements in the design of any infrastructure dedicated to a data environment.

Nonetheless, there a number of unique tasks that need to be completed in order to align the staging area to the ETL methodology discussed in prior sections of this chapter.

First, the data architect and the DBA will need to create separate environments for each stage that the data goes through. This means separate database and file systems that are dedicated to the stage that the ETL lifecycle is in.

For example, a devoted database instance and related file

systems should be created for the data acquisition and profiling stages. The tasks included in these stages are the reading of every data element and record in order to generate detailed statistical information on the source data. This means that processes involved in the profiling effort will be using tremendous amounts of resources related to memory and CPU and should be segregated so that other workloads are not adversely impacted. The design of the database instance must take into consideration the fact that with the use of federated data, there may be implications at the database level that will cause ripple effects on the other data objects within the database instance. Also the file systems allocated to the containers that the database uses should be separate from the file systems used in the data acquisition process so that there are no I/O bottleneck issues.

Then there is the SECURITY component! This is live production data that has highly sensitive information. This data cannot be masked and/or scrambled as this defeats the whole purpose of the ETL process to stage data into the data warehouse or ODS. The raw data must be exposed in order for the ETL to be as effective in integrating, cleansing and standardizing all data from all sources. Hence, having a strong security framework is an essential ingredient in this configuration. Typically, the data steward and an appointed business analyst should be among the chosen few that have access to some of the sensitive data elements. The ETL developers, DBA and system administrator does not need to see any of it. There is also the prevention of copying data. No one should be allowed to make copies of anything for any purpose. The data hub should be able to satisfy all requests for data access for analysis in a robustly secured environment.

CHAPTER 8
The Core Data Warehouse Layer

8.1 Core is core!

As a reminder, the IDH™ is not a Data Warehouse!

In fact, IDH™ is a lot more than a Data Warehouse; it is a Hub of Integrated Data and a Reference Architecture as well as a collection of best practices.

However, one of the main components of the IDH™ is called the Core Data Warehouse, why?

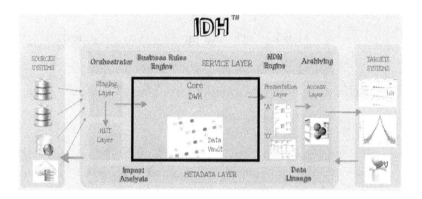

Figure 7 - The Core Data Warehouse Layer

This is simply because; this is the layer where you will find an integrated view of the Enterprise Data. As these data are also subject oriented, non-volatile and time-variant, we can consider that we are talking about a Data Warehouse, perfectly in-line with the Bill Inmon's definition.

In the Chapter 5, we learned that this reference architecture was thought to be most relevant to when:

- Your EDWH has to be fault resistant
- Your EDWH is supposed not to be impacted by changes in the surrounding environment, and particularly when new sources are added frequently or existing ones change often.
- Business rules are subject to change over time.
- Auditability is required.
- The structure of arrival data is not always known.
- Historization and time slices are required.

Our challenge here is to build a Core Data Warehouse Layer to cover all these requirements.

To achieve this important challenge, we will have to choose the best Data Modeling technique.

Data modeling is important because it specifies the data structure, which can impact all aspects of data usage. For example, it can have a significant impact on performance. This is particularly true with data warehousing. And, the data warehouse is the primary structural element in business intelligence.

Key to business intelligence is the ability to analyze huge volumes of data, typically by means of query processing and analytic applications. And for this, performance is critical.

8.2 The Importance of Data Modeling

Generally speaking, a model is an abstraction and reflection of the real world. Modeling gives us the ability to visualize what we cannot yet realize. It is the same with data modeling. The primary aim of a data model is to make sure that all data objects required by the business are accurately and fully represented.

From the business perspective, a data model can be easily verified because the model is built by using notations and language which are easy to understand and decipher.

However, from a technical perspective the data model is also detailed enough to serve as a blueprint for the database administrator (DBA) when building the physical database. For example, the model can easily be used to define the key elements, such as the primary keys, foreign keys, and tables that will be used in the design of the data structure.

Finally, a good data model is also a fantastic and powerful communication tool!

8.3 Different Approaches of Data Modeling

Data models are about capturing and presenting information. Every organization has information that is typically either in the operational form (such as OLTP applications) or the informational form (such as the data warehouse).

Traditionally, data modelers have made use of the Entity/Relationship diagram, developed as part of the data modeling process, as a communication media with the business analysts. The focus of the Entity/Relationship model is to capture the relationships between various entities of the organization or process for which we design the model.

The Entity/Relationship diagram is a tool that can help in the analysis of business requirements and in the design of the resulting data structure.

However, the focus of the dimensional model is on the business. Dimensional modeling gives us an improved capability to visualize the very abstract questions that the business analysts are required to answer. Utilizing dimensional modeling, analysts can easily understand and navigate the data structure and fully exploit the data. Actually, data is simply a record of all business activities, resources, and results of the organization. The data model is a well-organized abstraction of that data. So, it is quite natural that the data model has become the best method for understanding and managing the business of the organization.

Without a data model, it would be very difficult to organize the structure and contents of the data in the data warehouse.

Entity/Relationship and dimensional modeling, although related, are extremely different. Of course, all dimensional models are also really Entity/Relationship models. However, when we refer to Entity/Relationship models in this book, we mean normalized Entity/Relationship models. Dimensional models are denormalized.

There is much debate about which method is best and the conditions under which you should select a particular technique. People use Entity/Relationship modeling primarily when designing for highly transaction-oriented OLTP applications.

When working with data warehousing applications, Entity/Relationship modeling may be good for reporting and fixed queries, but dimensional modeling is typically better for ad hoc query and analysis.

For the OLTP applications, the goal of a well-designed Entity/Relationship data model is to efficiently and quickly get the data inside (Insert, Update, Delete) the database.

However, on the data warehousing side, the goal of the data model (Dimensional) is to get the data out (select/group by) of the warehouse.

Personally, I recommend another modeling technique, but let discuss it later…

8.4 Entity / Relationship Modeling and Third Normal Form

Normalization is the process of efficiently organizing data in a database. There are two goals of the normalization process: eliminating redundancy and ensuring data dependencies make sense.

> *Third normal form (3NF)* is the third step in normalizing a database and it builds on the first and second normal forms, 1NF and 2NF.
>
> *3NF* states that all column reference in referenced data that are not dependent on the primary key should be removed. Another way of putting this is that only foreign key columns should be used to reference

> *another table, and no other columns from the parent table should exist in the referenced table.*
>
> (Janssen, Cory, 2012)

Normalization, and in particular 3NF is used to design Operational Databases (On Line Transactional Processing). Online transaction processing, or OLTP, refers to a class of systems that facilitate and manage transaction-oriented applications, typically for data entry and retrieval transaction processing.

It means that these OLTP systems must be designed in order to facilitate the Insertion, deletion and update of a record without putting at risk the referential integrity of the data base.

3NF modeling is perfect to achieve this goal: As seen in the definition, in 3NF, all attributes of a table depends on the same key.

Example 1

CUSTOMER

CustID	Name	Surname	City	Post Code
12345	David	Gahan	London	SW7 2AP
67891	Martin	Gore	London	WC 2H7 Y
35421	Andrew	Fletcher	Coventry	CV4 7AL

Figure 8 - E/R Customer

This is not in strict 3NF as the City could be obtained from the Post code attribute. If you created a table containing postcodes then city could be derived.

CustomerID	Firstname	Surname	PostCode*
12345	David	Gahan	SW7 2AP
67891	Martin	Gore	WC2H 7JY
35421	Andrew	Fletcher	CV4 7AL

Figure 9 - E/R Customer 2

POSTCODES

PostCode	City
SW7 2AP	London
WC2H 7JY	London
CV4 7AL	Coventry

Figure 10 - E/R Post Codes

Example 2.

VideoID	Title	Certificate	Description
12345	Saw IV	18	Eighteen and over
67891	Igor	PG	Parental Guidance
35421	Bambi	U	Universal Classification

Figure 11 - E/R Films

The Description of what the certificate means could be obtained from the certificate attribute - it does not need to refer to the primary key VideoID. So split it out and use the primary key / secondary key approach.

Example 3

CLIENT

ClientID	CinemaID*	CinemaAddress
12345	LON23	1 Leicester Square. London
67891	COV2	34 Bramby St, Coventry
35421	MAN4	56 Croydon Rd, Manchester

Figure 12 - E/R Client

CINEMAS

CinemaID	CinemaAddress
LON23	1 Leicester Square. London
COV2	34 Bramby St, Coventry
MAN4	56 Croydon Rd, Manchester

Figure 13 - E/R Cinemas

In this case the database is almost in 3NF - for some reason the Cinema Address is being repeated in the Client table, even though it can be obtained from the Cinemas table. So simply remove the column from the client table

Example 4

ORDER

OrderID	Quantity	Price	Cost
12345	2	10.00	20.00
67891	3	20.00	60.00
35421	4	30.00	120.00

Figure 14 - E/R Order

In this case the cost of any order can be obtained by multiplying quantity by price. This is a 'calculated field'. The database is larger than it needs to be as a query could work out the cost of any order. So to be in strict 3NF you would remove the Cost column.

As we can see in the above examples, 3NF is perfect to manage data for operational systems, but it is not set to comply with EDW requirements. In particular, this modeling technique does not offer a solution for history tracking.

If you want to build an EDW using 3NF, you will have to create a technical key, also called surrogate key and add a Date/Time stamp to this surrogate key in order to enable historization. It is also better to add a field in order to track the data source.

Note that even if this modeling technique is possible for your EDW, you will be very strongly coupled with the design of your source systems.

Indeed, imagine that the structure of the tables of your source system change or even worse the whole system should be replaced by a brand new system, with a completely different table structure. The impact on the design of your EDW would be dreadful!

Not to mention that this kind of modeling is not made to be performant when we run large queries against it.

For all these reasons, I recommend to use 3NF to do the modeling of the staging layer or the ODS layer, but not for the Core Data Warehouse layer!

8.5 Dimensional Modeling

To overcome performance issues for large queries in the data warehouse, we use dimensional models. The dimensional modeling approach provides a way to improve query performance for summary reports without affecting data integrity. However, that performance comes with a cost for extra storage space.

A dimensional database generally requires much more space than its relational counterpart. However, with the ever decreasing costs of storage space, that cost is becoming less significant.

A dimensional model is also commonly called a star schema. This type of model is very popular in data warehousing because it can provide much better query performance, especially on very large queries, than an Entity/Relationship model. However, it also has the major benefit of being easier to understand. It consists, typically, of a large table of facts (known as a fact table), with a number of other tables surrounding it that contain descriptive data, called dimensions. When it is drawn, it resembles the shape of a star, therefore the name.

*In data warehousing and business intelligence (BI), a **star schema** is the simplest form of a dimensional model, in which data is organized into facts and dimensions.*

A fact is an event that is counted or measured, such as a sale or login. A dimension contains reference information about the fact, such as date, product, or customer. A star schema is diagramed by surrounding each fact with its associated dimensions. The resulting diagram resembles a star.

(Rouse, Margaret, 2010)

The dimensional model consists of two types of tables having different characteristics. They are:

> ➢ Fact table
>
> ➢ Dimension table

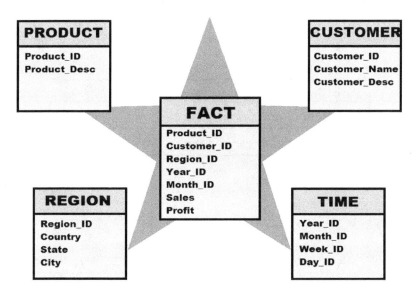

Figure 15 - Star Schema

The following sections provide more detail for understanding the two types of tables. **Figure 16** depicts an example of the fact table structure.

Fact table characteristics

- The fact table contains numerical values of what you measure. For example, a fact value of 20 might mean that 20 widgets have been sold.
- Each fact table contains the keys to associated dimension tables. These are called foreign keys in the fact table.
- Fact tables typically contain a small number of columns.
- Compared to dimension tables, fact tables have a large number of rows.

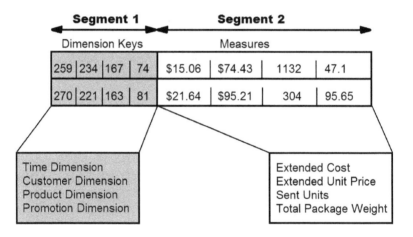

Figure 16 - Fact Table Structure

The information in a fact table has characteristics, such as:

- It is numerical and used to generate aggregates and summaries.
- Data values need to be additive or semi-additive, to

enable summarization of a large number of values.

- All facts in Segment 2 must refer directly to the dimension keys in Segment 1 of the structure, as you see in **Figure 16**. This enables access to additional information from the dimension tables.

We have depicted examples of a good fact table design and a bad fact table design in **Figure 17**. The bad fact table contains data that does not follow the basic rules for fact table design. For example, the data elements in this table contain values that are:

• Not numeric. Therefore, the data cannot be summarized.

• Not additive. For example, the discounts and rebates are hidden in the unit price.

• Not directly related to the given key structure, which means they cannot be not additive.

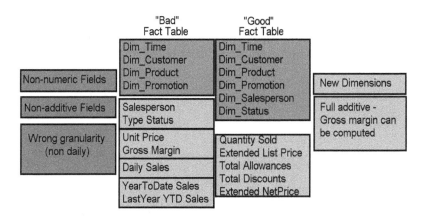

Figure 17 - Bad and Good Fact Tables

Dimension table characteristics

-   Dimension tables contain the details about the facts. That, as an example, enables the business analysts to better understand the data and their reports.

-   The dimension tables contain descriptive information about the numerical values in the fact table. That is, they contain the attributes of the facts. For example, the dimension tables for a marketing analysis application might include attributes such as time period, marketing region, and product type.

-   Since the data in a dimension table is denormalized, it typically has a large number of columns.

-   The dimension tables typically contain significantly fewer rows of data than the fact table.

-   The attributes in a dimension table are typically used as row and column headings in a report or query results display. For example, the textual descriptions on a report come from dimension attributes. **Figure 18** depicts an example of this.

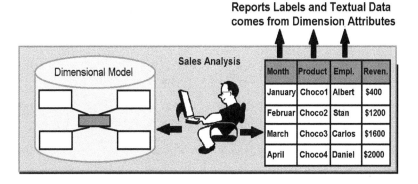

Figure 18 - The textual data in the report comes from dimension attributes

The word "Kimball" is synonymous with **dimensional modeling.** *Ralph didn't invent the original basic concepts of facts and dimensions, however, he established an extensive portfolio of dimensional techniques and vocabulary, including conformed dimensions, slowly changing dimensions, junk dimensions, mini-dimensions, bridge tables, periodic and accumulating snapshot fact tables, and the list goes on. Over the nearly 20 years, Ralph and his Kimball Group colleagues have written hundreds of articles and* Design Tips *on dimensional modeling, as well as the seminal text,* The Data Warehouse Toolkit, Second Edition *(John Wiley, 2002).*

(Ross, Margie, 2008)

8.6 Which model for your EDW?

Is the Entity/Relationship modeling the solution to design a Data Warehouse?

According to Bill Inmon, it is!

Indeed, Bill Inmon suggests that his Corporate Information Architecture is the EDW.

> *The* **Corporate Information Factory (CIF)** *is a logical architecture whose purpose is to deliver business intelligence and business management capabilities driven by data provided from business operations. The CIF has proven to be a stable and enduring technical architecture for any size enterprise desiring to build strategic and tactical decision support systems (DSSs). The CIF consists of producers of data and consumers of information.*
>
> (Imhoff, Claudia, 1999)

Of course, I like the Inmon's architecture. It is very simple to build and to load, but I am not convinced that this architecture will be adapted to help us with future challenges the BI world will face in the coming years.

Fortunately, Bill Inmon's thought continue to evolve in the right direction, and we will discuss these developments a later.

Is Dimensional Modeling the solution to design a Data Warehouse?

According to Ralph Kimball, it is!

Indeed, Ralph Kimball considers that the EDW is made of the collection of your star schemas. And with the extensive usage of conformed dimensions, you can build a Bus Matrix, which is your EDW.

> *A bus architecture is composed of a set of tightly integrated data marts that get their power from conformed dimensions and fact tables. A conformed dimension is defined and implemented one time, so that it means the same thing everywhere it's used. Fact tables that should be conformed include those that derive revenue, profit, standard prices, and standard costs.*
>
> (Poolet, Michelle A., 2007)

		CONFORMED DIMENSIONS								
		Date	Customer	Application	Transaction	Location	Device	Counter	Network Address	Supplier
SLA monitoring Systems	Network Performance	✓		✓		✓	✓		✓	
	Server Health	✓	✓	✓			✓	✓		
	User Experience Monitoring	✓	✓		✓	✓				
	Application Performance	✓	✓	✓	✓		✓			
	Application Discovery	✓	✓	✓		✓	✓			✓

Figure 19 - Bus Architecture and Conformed Dimensions

In fact I was an unconditional fan of Ralph Kimball, and I attended his training courses as often as I could, and I guess I am still fascinated by the man and his work.

I consider that dimensional modeling is the perfect and only solution, to build a performant source for analytical reporting and above all, it is a fantastic communication tool!

But, after so much time trying to build the perfect Inmon's EDW or Kimball DWH, my finding is implacable: The only EDW I succeeded to implement was always built on a hybrid architecture!

My opinion is that unlike Bill Inmon, who has been able to evolve his concept, Ralph Kimball fell asleep on its laurels and did not make new proposals since a long time.

8.7 Data Vault Modeling

As seen above, for many years, two classical visions clash in what concerns the modeling of Data Warehouses. The Inmon's approach by subject and normalized and the Kimball's approach using star schemas and where the integration into an Enterprise Data Warehouse is ensured by Conformed Dimensions and the use of a Matrix Bus.

Although less present than the two conventional approaches, there is a third way: the Data Vault modeling approach advocated by its inventor Dan Linstedt since the beginning of the 2000s.

Data Vault modeling is a kind of terraced approach between Inmon and Kimball.

> *Data Vault Modeling* is a database modeling method that is designed to provide long-term historical storage of data coming in from multiple operational systems. It is also a method of looking at historical data that, apart from the modeling aspect, deals with issues such as auditing, tracing of data, loading speed and resilience to change.
>
> *The Data Vault* is a detail oriented, historical tracking and uniquely linked set of normalized tables that support one or more functional areas of business. It is a hybrid approach encompassing the

best of breed between 3rd normal form (3NF) and star schema. The design is flexible, scalable, consistent and adaptable to the needs of the enterprise

(From Wikipedia, the free encyclopedia)

A Data Vault model is composed of three types of entities: the Hubs, Links and Satellites.

The Hubs are business concepts. These entities contain natural keys (business keys) that identify the concept and which are inherently very stable. They contain no data that describes the entity (these are kept in the Satellite entities described below). They are often the point of connection (hence the term 'hub') among several sectors of an organization. **Figure 20** shows an example of model Data Vault. Entities Position, used, display position and Application are hubs.

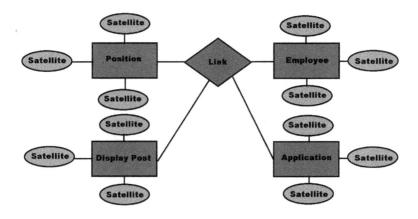

Figure 20 - Data Vault Model example

The Links are associative entities. They bind together at least two Hubs; in other words, they are in relation to business concepts. The entity link employee-Application of **figure 20** is an example of a link.

Satellites contain data describing the hubs and links at any given time and through time. These entities contain the context (from business process) of a hub or a link. As descriptive data changes often, the idea of satellites is to preserve changes when they occur. As its name suggests, a satellite is a dependent entity in relation to a hub or a link. Conversely, a hub must always contain at least one satellite to describe it.

One of the central ideas of a Data Vault model is to separate the structural data (Hubs and Links between the

Hubs) of the descriptive data that define the context of these data (Satellites). Structural concepts of an organization are thus separated from the contexts of use of these concepts.

Another central idea of a Data Vault model is that it keeps intact the context of source systems. The data coming from the sources are integrated into a raw Data Vault type warehouse without transformations (beyond integration and hisorization). The data are therefore loaded quickly in their raw format including the date and the source of loading. It is therefore possible to reconstruct the image of a source at any moment in time. Not transforming the data is one of the fundamental differences with two conventional approaches. It is said that a Data Vault Warehouse is a warehouse that can represent raw data (Raw Data Warehouse) and also can represent a business integrated view of data (Business DataWarehouse).

The Data Vault approach offers several advantages:

- It is flexible and resistant to change.
- It is extensible.
- Changes in the sources are quickly reflected in the warehouse.
- It makes it easy to restore an image of source data to any moment in time.

8.8 A Closer Look at the DV Hubs

A hub contains a natural key to identify uniquely (at least, it is hoped!) an instance of a business concept. A natural key is a key which is visible and used by the organization to identify an instance of a concept. As an example, the employee number is used to uniquely identify an employee in different contexts/processes: human resources, management of parking lots, incidents, payroll, financial system... The employee number is therefore the point of connection (communication) of the 'employee' concept between different business units, Hence the name Hub.

---

*In relational model database design, a **natural key** is a key that is formed of attributes that already exist in the real world. For example, a USA citizen's social security number could be used as a natural key. In other words, a natural key is a candidate key that has a logical relationship to the attributes within that row. A natural key is sometimes called a domain key.*

(From Wikipedia, the free encyclopedia)

A natural key is different from internal identifiers of the source systems that are, in principle, non-visible and specific to the system that generates the values.

In an ideal world, every concept would be associated to the same key, regardless of the business unit, and the key would be unique. In practice, it is far from being always the case. For example, the management of incidents could use its own natural key for various resources involved.

> ***The job of a Hub*** *is to track the first time the Data Vault sees a Business Key arrive in the Warehousing load, and where it came from.*
>
> ***The Purpose of a Hub*** *is to provide a soft-integration point of raw data that is not altered from the source system, but is supposed to have the same semantic meaning.*
>
> (Linstedt, Dan, 2010)

Here are criteria to meet in order to be a good Hub.

A Hub:

- Represents one and only one single concept;
- Contains no descriptive data elements (example: the name of an employee). A Hub' satellites contain the descriptive part;
- Contains no relationship. The Links contain relations between the hubs and satellites contain relations between the description of a concept and the

concept (Hub) described;

- Ideally contains a unique natural key consisting of at least a data element that identifies the concept (example: the number of the parking lot). For example, if in two sources, a same natural key value does not match the same instance of a concept, you must uniquely identify the different instances using the natural key combined with the name of the source (or division, department, country,etc.) where the data comes from.

- Always contains at least two attributes of information allowing for the traceability: the source where the data came from and when the data was brought in the hub (Time Stamp).

- Is associated with at least one satellite to describe.

- Contains a Hub Sequence Id

The Hub Sequence Id is a Data Warehouse created and managed primary key sequence ID. This is the key that will be used to form key constraints. The Hub Sequence ID has a one-to-one (1:1) relationship with the Natural Business Key of the Hub.

(Hultgren, Hans, 2012)

8.9 A Closer Look to the Links

A link is a dependent entity representing an interaction between at least two concepts which it depends.

As in the case of a star model, the granularity of a link (level of detail) is dictated by the hubs in connection with the link.

> ***The Link*** *represents the relationship… between two or more business components (two or more business keys).*
>
> (Linstedt, Dan, 2004)

Here are criteria to meet in order to be a good link.

A link:

- Is associated with at least two parent concepts (Hubs) (Note: in the case of a hierarchical link or same-as link it can associate two times with the same Hub);
- Contains no descriptive data elements (example: begin date and end date of the relationship). Link Satellites contain the descriptive part;
- Is the only type of entities containing the relationship between concepts;

- Is used regardless of the cardinality of the relationship between two concepts. It does not consider cardinalities more specific than a relationship many-to-many. So, a change in cardinality will not affect the model (Note: a more specific cardinality rule can be documented at the metadata level);

- Always contains at least two attributes of information allowing for the traceability: the source from which comes the link and when the instance of the link led in the warehouse (Time Stamp);

- Is implemented by foreign keys that point to the identifiers (internal) of the hubs in the relationship;

- Is defined with the finest possible grain, except for redundant Links defined at a higher granularity for performance reasons;

- Is created if the grain changes and the old link remains in order to avoid the re-engineering of the existing model and ensures auditability.

The **Link** *has its own* **Sequence ID** *just has the Bub does. The cardinality between this Link Sequence ID must ne one-to-one (1:1) with a single instance of the natural business relationship.*

(Hultgren, Hans, 2012)

Several of these criteria are ensuring that the existing structure of the model structure does not need reengineering when changes occur in the business environment.

The structure of the Data Vault model is designed so that when changes occur, they have no impact on the existing parts of the model. Links are added without revising the existing structures. The structure is therefore flexible and new information are added with much less effort. There is no need of conversion of existing data in the new structure.

Concerning the quote from Dan Linstedt about the definition of a Link:

Today there is some confusion on the Link being used (by itself) to represent a transaction. Actually a transaction is also a form of business concept and so it also has a Hub (some form of key). Since a Link is only the association/relationship between two things, and because it only tracks the first time this association/relationship is seen by the data warehouse, it could not track for example recurring transactions without some key as a tie-breaker. Since a Link does not have its own business key (only FKs) it must then get another key from another Hub. This other Hub would represent the Transaction concept/entity.

8.10 A Closer Look to the Satellites

A satellite is a dependent entity containing detailed information about a hub or a link. It contains the history of changes of the descriptive and contextual information. Somehow, we can say that it is the Data Warehouse part of the Data Vault model.

Figure 21 shows an example of satellites. Employee Hub is described by two Satellites: a Satellite employee name containing the personal information of the employee and a Satellite employee that contains the addresses coordinated and numbers where to join the employee.

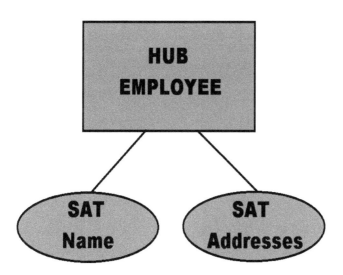

Figure 21 - Examples of Satellites

Here are criteria to meet in order to be a good satellite.

A satellite:

- Is on a dependent relationship with one and only one single Hub or one and only one single Link; The relationship is established by a foreign key that points to the internal identifier of the Hub or the Link to which it belongs;

- Is never in connection with another Satellite (i.e., a Satellite is never the parent of a relationship);

- Can be divided in different Satellites, by type (classification), rate of change (data that change at a different pace are separated to avoid the redundancy of data that change less rapidly) and data source to simplify the loading;

- Always contains at least two attributes of information allowing for the traceability: the source from which comes the description and when the descriptive instance was brought in the warehouse (Time Stamp);

- Contains all context and all of the historization of the data warehouse.

> *The Satellite inherits the* **Sequence ID** *of the Natural Business Concept or Relationship that it will describe.*
>
> *The Satellite does not have its own* **Sequence ID.**
>
> *Together the* **Sequence ID FK and the Load Date/Time Stamp** *form the Primary Key (PK) of a Satellite*
>
> (Hultgren, Hans, 2012)

For performance reasons, it is sometimes desirable to regroup in a snapshot taken at a regular interval (example: daily) the key of the parent table and the loading date of the current instance (at the time of the snapshot) for each of the satellites of the same parent. This approach provides a consolidated view of satellites and simplifies their querying (although querying is not the primary purpose of a warehouse of raw data...). This structure is called PIT for 'Point In Time'. In our example, we could use a 'PIT employee' table containing the Hub employee internal ID and the dates of last load of the two satellites together with the date of snapshot.

Finally let's mention another grouping in snapshot called 'Bridge', also used for reasons of performance and ease of access, combining this time of hubs, links and potentially some satellite attributes in one single structure.

8.11 Business Key Alignment

The Business Key is the most important concept to deal with when we start modeling a Data Vault Data Warehouse.

> *At the core of the Data Vault is the Hub which we refer to as the* **business key**.
>
> (Hultgren, Hans, 2012)

When you start modeling with Data Vault, you have to go back to the business analysis to collect business requirements for of given subject area, and from there, identify the Hubs.

Once the Hubs are defined, you should identify the natural business relationships between these Hubs to design the Links, and finally you must collect the contextual information, their rate of change and their sources, in order to design the Satellites.

Do not forget that all the identified core business concepts are supposed to become Hubs. In other words, a Business Key is representative of the core business entity like "customer" or "product" for example. But the Business Key also represents event based keys. Think about the Core Business Concepts such as "Sales" for example.

As when we design our Data Vault Data Warehouse, we will discuss with the Business about end to end processes, the Business Key that we will discover should also be meaningful across the enterprise. These Business Keys are referred as Enterprise Wide Business Keys (EWBK).

The main purpose of the IDH™ is to integrate data coming from different sources, so by definition, the arriving keys are not always fully aligned with these EWBK.

It is thus important to align the Business Keys in order to perform the requested integration across the enterprise.

Since we are typically dealing with hundreds of sources, each commonly subject to updates and changes, we should not plan to model our EDW using keys driven by a subset of these source systems.

(Hultgren, Hans, 2012)

In a traditional Data Warehousing approach, we would be tempted to perform the Business Key alignment in the Data Mart Layer, using conformed dimension for example. But As a Data Mart has a departmental scope, the risk here is to lose our aim of having am integration across the whole enterprise and finally to have to maintain data silos.

Another problem we have to face is the contradiction between our requirement to have a Core Data Warehouse with all the data loaded to be a mirror of the sources, and the need to have a Core Data Warehouse aligned with the organizational view of the business keys and if possible, the business terms.

Let's take an example to illustrate what we just said.

<u>**NOTA**</u>: I have to be honest here, and mention that all the explanation on the Business Key alignment is directly inspired and sometime copied directly from the book of Hans Hultgren: Modeling The Agile Data Warehouse With Data Vault.

Thank you again Hans for your help!

Imagine that we have a central Data Warehouse that has a core business concept of 'Customer'. There is information concerning Customers available in several source systems. But these sources have variations on this business concept- The sources have concepts of 'Users', 'Customer' and 'Person'.

The concept of 'User' is a form of super-set of 'Customer'. For these systems you cannot be a 'Customer' without being a 'User', however you can be a 'User' and not be a 'Customer'.

The concept of 'Customer' in the case of the second source

system is in fact the same as the central definition of the 'Customer' core business concept.

The concept of 'Person' coming from the last source is a bit more confused. A 'Person' can really be anything, anyone. In the 'Person' feed from this source are Customers, Employees, Vendors, Partners, Prospects and Leads.

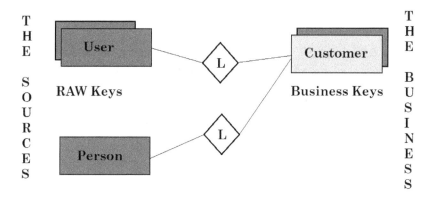

Figure 22 - Source Vs Central Key

To deal with these in the Data Warehouse we need to persist data in tables designed around 'User' and 'Person'. We have to do this because if we apply the soft business rule to translate them to 'Customer' records, we will lose auditability and traceability of data. Also, we would not be able to respond to a change in the transformation business rules since the source representation of the data would no longer be available.

In this case then we load the 'User' and 'Person' data into

their own structures (note that multiple source systems loaded the 'User' table structures since they were aligned with each other), we load the 'Customer' data directly into 'Customer' (because that source was already aligned).

We apply the business rules to transform the Users and Customers into 'Customer' records, and lastly we create links to show the lineage of 'Customer' records to their corresponding 'User' or 'Person' records.

Now the 'User' and the 'Person' Table structures are part of the RAW Data Warehouse components and the Customer is part of the Business Data Warehouse (BDW) components.

This is true for all such key alignment activities.

Note that the 'Customer' contains at least some records that are both RAW (directly traceable) and BDW. But it is placed in the RAW Layer because at least some records are the product of soft Business Rule transformations.

Note also that the source of each record is still available in the Record Source attribute which accompanies all records in all Data Vault tables. So we can always discern which records were **Sysgen** (system generated by us – we created the records based on business rules) versus those that came directly from a source feed.

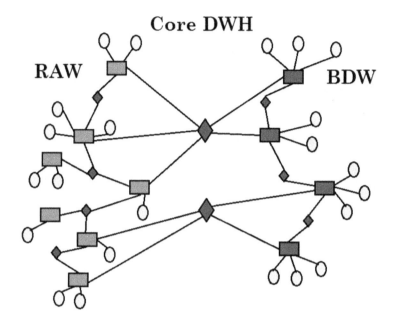

Figure 23 - RAW & BDW in the Core DWH

8.12 Data Vault As A Key Success Factor For The IDH

If you have read this book until here, you are certainly now familiar with the concept of Integrated Data Hub™, and when and why you should adopt this reference architecture!

But a small reminder is always welcome, right?

This IDH reference architecture was thought to be most relevant to when:

- Your EDWH has to be fault resistant
- Your EDWH is supposed not to be impacted by changes in the surrounding environment, and particularly when new sources are added frequently or existing ones change often.
- Business rules are subject to change over time.
- Auditability is required.
- The structure of arrival data is not always known.
- Historization and time slices are required

As the Data Vault experts you are now, you will easily agree with me that Data Vault Modeling is the perfect modeling methodology of the Core Data Warehouse Layer of the IDH, as it allows us to meet almost all the requirements listed above!

And obviously, the insensitivity to changes in the structures of the source data is really one strong point of the Data Vault methodology.

The fact that the contextual information can be split by rate of change and data source is also a fantastic advantage.

And, imagine! All the data are loaded into the Data Vault. Nothing is rejected. In terms of fault resistance, can we imagine a better solution?

And think about Data Lineage and Auditability! As we store a Record Source and a Time Stamp in each records of each table in our Data Vault, the lineage is maintained automatically!

For all these reasons, I am convinced that the extensive usage of Data Vault Modeling for the Core Data Warehouse Layer of the IDH is a Key Success Factor!

In the next chapters I will talk about a lot of other important concepts behind the IDH. The sum of all these concepts makes the IDH the Next Generation Data Warehouse. The only one architecture able to face the future challenges of Data Integration!

CHAPTER 9
The HiST Layer

9.1 An Optional Layer?

If your strategy requires you to be able to reload your Data Warehouse from scratch, or if you need to be able to replay the last loads, I strongly advise you to include this layer in your architecture!

This will also be the only place where you will find a trace of the data that were one day present on your decommissioned sources.

I am sure that you already faced the challenge to rebuild your Data Warehouse, while your legacy sources are not present anymore! If not, be sure that it will be the case one day…

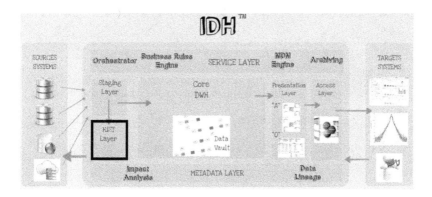

Figure 24 - The HiST Layer

So, think twice before considering this layer as optional,

because once your decision is taken and implemented, there is no way back!

9.2 Historization Of The Staging

In the IDH™ Reference Architecture, HiST stands for Historization of the Staging.

What does it mean exactly?

In fact this is certainly the easiest IDH™ concept to understand and to implement!

It is just to keep an image of the data passed through the staging tables. In doing this, we have very simple and efficient way to replay on or several load, including with data that are not present anymore in your source systems.

Of course, you should think about an archiving and back-up strategy to avoid storing tons of very old data, but the idea here is to be able to reload your Data Warehouse at any point in time.

In case of corruption of your Core Data Warehouse, the simplest solution should be to restore a backup of the EDW data, and to replay the needed historized staging that you fortunately stored in your HiST layer!

9.3 This is not an ODS!

In a traditional EDW reference architecture, you should find something called Operational Data Store (ODS) exactly at the place where I have put my HiST layer. But be careful, the HiST layer is not an ODS!

The HiST layer is not a good place to do Operational Reporting. The data are not integrated and the real historization is not yet performed.

> *Operational reporting* is designed to support the detailed day-to-day activities of the corporation at the transaction level. In operational reporting, detail is much more important than summary. In fact, in operational reporting summary information is often irrelevant.
>
> Examples of operational reporting include bank teller end-of-day window balancing reports, daily account audits and adjustments, daily production records, flight-by-flight traveler logs and transaction logs.
>
> (Inmon, Bill, 2000)

In fact there is no ODS in the IDH™ Reference

Architecture. The Operational Reporting is performed elsewhere, but this will be tone of the topic of the next chapter.

CHAPTER 10
The Presentation Layer

10.1 A Multi-Purpose Layer

The aim of the presentation layer is to host the data, (or should I say the information?) which will be presented to the consumer.

I used the word consumer on purpose, as the IDH is not only a Corporate Data Warehouse aiming to prepare the data to be consumed by end-users, but also information to be consumed by other operational or analytical applications.

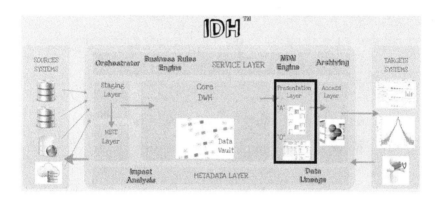

Figure 25 - The Presentation Layer

As the information can be presented to a user willing to do analytical or operational reporting or to an application, the presentation layer must have different type of data structures, each one adapted to the final usage of these information.

This is why in the IDH™ Reference Architecture, in the Presentation Layer, you will find two different types of data structures. Respectively the "A" type and the "O" type.

I suppose that you already guessed that "A" stands for Analytical and "O" is for Operational…

10.2 The What? And The Why?

A corporate data warehouse must allow users to answer to two types of questions.

The "What?" question is asked when the user wants to know the content of a database. The result is generally a list or a number.

An example of a "What?" question could be: "What is the list, or the number, of my employees with a driver license?"

The "Why?" question, on the other hand, arises when the user wishes to explore the data that are available to him looking for a response. Usually the information is provided on an aggregated way.

A good example of a "Why?" question is: "Why do I lose money, on this type of product, in this geographical area, compared to last year?"

10.3 The "A" Type Presentation Layer

Of course, as we have corporate validated information in our Core Data Warehouse Layer, we can build a Presentation Layer destined to enable the end-user to perform analytical reporting. In other words to answer the "Why?" question.

As seen in Chapter 8, there exists an adapted data structure for each kind of usage.

Despite the slight criticisms that I have done on Ralph Kimball's work in a previous chapter, I still believe that star schemas are best suited to meet queries destined for Analytical Reporting.

This is why I propose in the Presentation Layer of the IDH™ Reference Architecture to use a Dimensional Modeling approach to store the data needed to answer business questions.

A data structure dedicated to answer a business question is called a Data Mart.

We will thus find in the Presentation Type « A » a collections of Kimball's style star schemas and OLAP Cubes.

> *An* **OLAP cube** *is a method of storing data in a multidimensional form, generally for reporting purposes. In OLAP cubes, data (measures) are categorized by dimensions.*
>
> **OLAP cubes** *are often pre-summarized across dimensions to drastically improve query time over relational databases. The query language used to interact and perform tasks with OLAP cubes is multidimensional expressions (MDX).*
>
> (Rouse, Margaret, 2012)

Let's be clear here. When I propose to adopt the Dimensional Modeling approach in the Type "A" Presentation Layer, I am not talking about adopting the whole Ralph Kimball's methodology and to rebuild a second enterprise Data Warehouse.

By the way you could opt to directly generate your OLAP cubes from the Data Vault or even to virtualize completely the "Type A" presentation Layer.

In the chapter dealing with new concepts, I will present more deeply these two last possibilities.

10.4 The "O" Type Presentation Layer

We saw before that the IDH™ Reference Architecture has no ODS Layer.

We would however like to offer to the user a place dedicated to operational reporting. In other words, to answer the "What?" question.

In the same way that we have decided to build a dedicated data structure to host the data needed to perform analytical reporting, my advice is to build a separated data structure dedicated to the operational reporting.

Here you have the possibility to use different kind of data modeling methodologies, but flat-table database is probably the most efficient solution.

> *A **flat-table database** is one that uses a single table to store all relevant data.*

You can use the same approach to store data destined to be sent to another application or to produce exchanges files.

CHAPTER 11
The Access Layer

11.1 A Single Point Of Access for A Single Version Of The Truth

Now that the row data are transformed in validated information in our Core Data Warehouse Layer, and stored in a convenient way for either reporting or analysis, let's our consumers access it.

In the IDH™ Reference Architecture, the Access Layer is meant to give our consumer a single point of access.

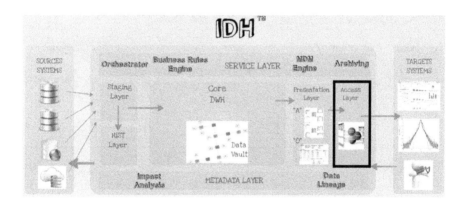

Figure 26 - The Access Layer

11.2 Corporate Business View

The data are now presented in a convenient structure to ease the queries to run against it.

But we all know that business users are not used to all deal with the same terms (vocabulary) and even less with some technical terms. This is why we need to translate the technical information into meaningful business information.

The layer where the information is translated into business terms is called Semantic Layer.

> *A **semantic layer** is a business representation of corporate data that helps end users access data using common business terms.*
>
> *The aim is to insulate users from the technical details of the data store and allow them to create queries in terms that are familiar and meaningful*
>
> (From Wikipedia, the free encyclopedia)

You have two choices here. Either you consider that the semantic layer is the IDH™ Access Layer or you build a separate one.

Most of reporting tools have their own semantic layer. If your company is using several different reporting tools, you most probably have to maintain all these semantic layers!

My advice is thus to build a unique Corporate Semantic Layer.

There is many ways to build this Corporate Semantic Layer; you can choose to buy a dedicated specialized software to do this, to use one of your reporting tools as the master repository for your business terms, or to use the database capabilities to manage your unique Corporate Semantic Layer.

A semantic layer has to be able to create technically sophisticated SQL and in many instances may need to generate multiple SQL statements in order to return the correct results (chasm trap/fan trap).

> The **Chasm trap** occurs when two "many to one" joins converge on a single table. For example a customer can place many orders/ and or place many loans.
>
> The **Fan trap** occurs when a "one to many" join links a table which is in turn linked by another "one to many" join.

The semantic layer must understand how to deal with database loops, complex objects, complex sets (union, intersect, minus), aggregate table navigation and shortcut joins.

CHAPTER 12
The Metadata Layer

12.1 Data About Data

The formal definition of the term Metadata is "Data About Data".

Ralph Kimball describes metadata as the DNA of the data warehouse as metadata defines the elements of the data warehouse and how they work together. He refers to three main categories of metadata: Technical metadata, business metadata and process metadata. Technical metadata are primarily definitional, while business metadata and process metadata are primarily descriptive.

Technical metadata *define the objects and processes in a DW/BI system, as seen from a technical point of view. The technical metadata include the system metadata which define the data structures such as: tables, fields, data types, indexes and partitions in the relational engine, and databases, dimensions, measures, and data mining models. Technical metadata define the data model and the way it is displayed for the users, with the reports, schedules, distribution lists and user security rights.*

Business metadata *are a content from the data warehouse described in more user-friendly terms. The business metadata tell you what data you have, where they come from, what they mean and what is their relationship is to other data in the data warehouse. Business metadata may also serve as a documentation for the DW/BI system. Users who browse the data warehouse are primarily viewing the business metadata.*

Process metadata *are used to describe the results of various operations in the data warehouse. Within the ETL process, all key data from tasks are logged on execution. This includes start time, end time, CPU seconds used, disk reads, disk writes and rows processed. When troubleshooting the ETL or query process, this sort of data becomes valuable. Process metadata are the fact measurement when building and using a DW/BI system. Some organizations make a living out of collecting and selling this sort of data to companies - in that case the process metadata become the business metadata for the fact and dimension tables. Collecting process metadata is in the interest of business people who can use the data to identify the users of their products, which products they are using and what level of service they are receiving.*

(Wikipedia, The Free Encyclopedia)

In the IDH™ Reference Architecture, you will find a Metadata Layer. This layer is designed to store all kinds of Metadata.

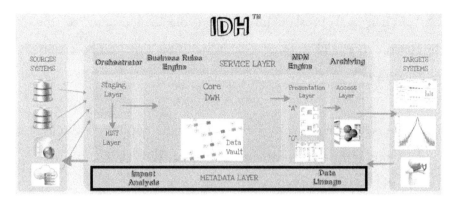

Figure 27 - The Metadata Layer

The Metadata Layer of the IDH™ is a transversal layer. It means that unlike the layers we have studied in the previous chapter, this one is a horizontal layer, while the others were presented as vertical.

The objective of this layer is to enable two important features of the IDH™, The Data Lineage and the Impact Analysis.

12.2 Data Lineage

I suppose that most data warehouse developers have already experienced the challenge of answering a question like "what data source fields are we using for this measure?" and you can even add "and what are we doing to it in the ETL process?"

When you present information or an indicator to the consumer, you have to provide at the same time the possibility to analyze and understand that information.

We saw in the previous chapter that the consumers can ask two important types of question to your EDWH. The "Why?" and the "What?" questions.

We are indeed supposed to give access to validated information but also to provide the consumer with a way to answer these two questions.

At the beginning of the Business Intelligence era, the only possibility provided to the consumer to answer their questions was to allow them to dig into the data.

By creating hierarchies in the data, and providing tools to drill down into the data, the users were able to start questioning the data in order to find a reliable answer.

---

*In information technology, to **drill down** means to move from summary information to detailed data by focusing in on something. In a GUI-environment, "drilling-down" may involve clicking on some representation in order to reveal more detail*

(Wikipedia, The Free Encyclopedia)

I personally believe that most of the time, the answer to the users' questions is not in the data itself!

It is most likely that if a flag is set to "red" in a user dashboard, the reason will be found somewhere in the metadata you collected during the loading phase of your Data Warehouse.

So, it is very important to also transform these metadata into meaningful and validated information in order to present it to the users.

Indeed, the flag is perhaps set to "red" because one of the business rules was violated? Or one of the data source was not available at the time of the load?

__Data lineage__ is generally defined as a kind of data life cycle that includes the data's origins and where it moves over time. This term can also describe what happens to data as it goes through diverse processes. Data lineage can help with efforts to analyze how information is used and to track key bits of information that serve a particular purpose.

(Techopedia.com - The IT Education Site)

If you correctly link your Metadata together, you will be able to offer the possibility to the user to navigate these Metadata and to offer him an easy way to understand how an indicator was build, why a flag is red or which version of which Business Rule was applied to these data.

In the Chapter titled "New Concepts" I will explain how to populate and link together automatically these Metadata.

12.3 Impact Analysis

If you organize correctly your Metadata, you will provide to the user an ability to find an answer to some of his questions, but you can also provide the DWH Managers with a fantastic tool to help them maintain the IDH and to propagate changes.

Imagine that each time a modification of the structure of the source data is changing or each time a transformation Business Rule is updated, you automatically know the impact that these changes on all your reports, KPIs, Dashboards, etc.

This automatic analysis is called Impact Analysis.

With a good reporting tool, you will be able to design fantastic reports showing the full Data Lineage and Impact Analysis from your Metadata Layer. If your tool has Drill Down capabilities, it is even better.

You can also imagine opting for a Data Vault Model for your Metadata. It is up to you to decide, but keep in mind that these two important concepts that are Data Lineage and Impact Analysis are crucial functionalities of the IDH.

You certainly already understood that these Metadata are also very useful when you are audited. More and more companies are supposed to be compliant with a lot of regulations. And when these companies are audited, the linkage between the Metadata are playing a crucial role.

If you are able to do it, my advice would be that you choose to upload to your Metadata Layer, all the information available in different repositories of the tools you used to document your sources data, the repositories of your ETL tool if you have one, and the repository of your Front End tools.

Another important source of your Metadata Layer is the data collected at the physical layers, like information about the memory of your servers, the consumption and usage of the processors, the disks statistics, etc.

The linkage of the externally generated Metadata and those generated during the loading phase of the IDH™ represents a fantastic source of information for the IDH™ administrators, but also for your Business Users.

Section III

Where we speak about New Concepts

CHAPTER 13
Logical Units of Work

13.1 The End of the Spaghettis

The code developed to load a Data Warehouse is called ETL Code. ETL stands for "Extraction, Transformation and Load".

These three steps are always present in a piece of DWH Code. Indeed, you always need to connect to a data source, to transform the data, even if the transformation is only a formatting, and then to load the results into a DWH table.

You can find a lot of tools in the market that will help you develop your ETL Code. By extension these tools are called ETL tools.

In these ETL tools you will hopefully find a lot of reusable components to help you deal with the most common transformations an ETL developer has to face when manipulating the data inside a DWH.

Sorting, pivoting, grouping, testing and ranking are among the most common transformations applied to the data during the ETL process. But after the application of these standard and simple manipulations, you will probably have to transform these data into validated information by applying Enterprise Business Rules to it.

And in the final step of your transformation process, you will normally want to compute some calculations in order to provide to the End User some facts and measures. These Measures are also called "Indicators" or "Key Performance Indicators".

Usually, the Presentation Layer of your DWH will be composed of a collection of Star Schemas, with the collections of the Measures stored in the Fact Table.

It is not uncommon to find more than 30 measures in a single Fact Table.

The temptation to write a single piece of ETL code preforming the connections to the source tables, the formatting transformations, the calculation of all the measures and finally the load of the results in the target tables is huge!

And imagine then on top of doing all the preceding transformation, your ETL Code is counting the number of treated rows, measuring the time between two actions, verifying that the external environment is ready to take some actions enabling it to continue working correctly, collecting the data from the different repositories and finally loading all these information to the Metadata Layer!

This is what I call a Spaghetti Code!

The Spaghetti Code is the nightmare of every EDH administrator.

You will find a lot of possible points of failure during the execution of this spaghetti code, and with of lot of luck, the ETL process will complete all the actions on time, with no errors.

But if an error occurs during the ETL process, it is likely that the result will be the loading of some incomplete information.

The only action you could take in case of error, is to restore a backup of the corrupted tables and to re-launch the spaghetti code, crossing your fingers that next time it will complete with no errors.

13.2 The Logical Unit of Work

For all the reasons evocated in the previous section, my advice is to put in place a development framework with guidelines and best practices.

One of these best practices should be to write small and independent pieces of ETL code; each piece of code doing very simple transformations.

In the IDH™ Reference Architecture and Best Practices, I call these small ETL pieces of code "Logical Unit of Work" or LUW.

A Logical Unit of Work is the greatest piece of code an ETL Developer is authorized to write.

When writing a LUW, an ETL developer has to keep in mind three important principles. These three principles are part of the IDH™ Reference Architecture and are called "Restartability", "Parallelism" and "Border to Border Scope".

13.3 Restartability

A Logical Unit of Work must be restartable!

Restartable means that if it fails, an external service should be able to restart this LUW automatically.

We will discuss about the notion of "services" later in this book.

To be restartable, a logical Unit of Work must be atomic and transactional, in other words a LUW is never incomplete. Either it is successfully terminated, or it is failed and it will be aborted and if possible it will be restarted.

It is up to you to describe in your ETL Framework and Best Practices all the development guidelines you want your ETL development team to apply.

13.4 Parallelism

A Logical Unit of Work must be parallelizable!

Parallelizable means that a LUW should be launch several times in parallel, or must be able to run at the same time as another LUW.

Here also, you have to describe, depending of the Operating System you are using and the Data Base hosting your systems, the best way to make it possible.

Your ETL Development team will have to keep in mind, when developing LUW, that to be parallelizable, a code should take the most important care on how the locks are managed and the flags are set.

13.5 Border to Border Scope

We have seen in the previous sections that a LUW should be restartable, parallelizable, atomic and transactional. I will add now another important concept.

The Logical Unit of Work must have a Border to Border scope!

Border to Border scope means that the scope of a LUW is to transport the data from one border of an IDH™ layer to the opposite layer of the same IDH™ layer.

In other words, it means that the LUW should only take care of the transport of the information from one border to the opposite border of an IDH™ layer¨. We have transformed the "T" of ETL from transformation to transport? Not exactly, but this will be explain later.

CHAPTER 14
The Service Layer

14.1 At Your Service!

In the previous chapter we have seen, that to avoid the nightmare of Spaghetti Code, you have to define a very strong ETL Development Framework. We have also seen the importance of defining small restartable, parallelizable piece of code, that I call Logical Unit of Work.

A LUW should be atomic with a border to border scope.

"All tasks, except the transport of the data from one border of a layer to the opposite border of the same layer, should be processed by an external service".

This is a very important sentence! But what does it mean exactly?

It simply means that, as you have certainly learned when you started to develop code, that a calculation, or in our case a transformation, should be performed by a function.

Sound familiar? I hope so!

If like me you started your developer carrier by using a procedural language, you are certainly used to call procedures and functions. Sometimes these functions are provided by the development tool itself; sometime you had to write your own functions.

Why should we do differently when developing ETL Code?

So my advice here is to manage all the transformations applied on the data during the ETL phase, in external functions. But as we are now in the Service era, I decided to call these external functions "services".

The advantage of externalizing your transformations to a service is the same that we have when calling a function or a procedure: The code of the transformation is centrally stored and managed. It helps you guarantee the Single Version of the Truth, by implementing a Single Version of the Code!

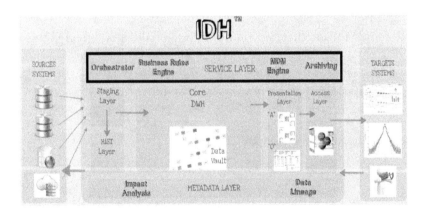

Figure 28 - The Service Layer

14.2 Business Rules Engine

To transform Data into Validated Information, you will have to apply to these data some calculations, filters, formatting etc.

The transformation are usually owned and defined by the business.

Let's take the example of a web based retail company.

One of the most important KPI (Key Performance Indicator) is certainly the Average Basket of a customer.

Behind this important indicator, you will probably find a formula, sometime, very complex, defining exactly how is calculated the Average Basket.

This formula is commonly called Business Rule.

This Business Rule should be defined owned and maintained by the business. In our example, probably the Sales and Marketing department.

With our definition of the LUW and the usage of the externalization of the transformations to an external service, we can implement easily the principle of Business Ownership of these transformations.

These Business Rules will most probably evolve over time.

In a Data Warehouse we have to take care of the historization of the data, and as we are supposed to rebuild completely our Data Warehouse from scratch. It is thus important to be able to apply an old version of a Business Rule to an ancient data to have a correct image of the past.

By applying the externalization of your Business Rules to a service, and using the concept of LUW, your ETL become very simple to write, manage and monitor.

ETL should now looks like E; T(BR#, Date);L.

If we push this concept a bit further, you could develop a Business Rules Engine. Or you could decide to buy one.

A Business Rules Engine should give your business the possibility to define, manage and monitor their Business Rules and to expose these Business Rules as service, so other application, like our LUWs, could call these services.

A good Business Rules engine should be usable by a Business User.

Imagine the Owner of a Business Rule going on the Corporate Intranet, to describe his Business Rule in a natural language, adding a validity date and publishing the rule as a service!

You think that this is only a dream? No! I have already developed and implemented this concept a couple of times, and I can ensure you, that it is totally feasible and that it will change dramatically the lives of your Business Users, of your ETL developers, your DWH administrators, an most important, will guarantee the Single Version of the Truth! And if I am not wrong, this what we are supposed to do, right?

14.3 Data Profiling, Data Formatting, Data Cleansing.

You can apply these principles of externalization of the transformation rules to any king of transformations.

Before applying Business Rules to transform your data to Indicators, you probably started in a previous layer, by applying some formatting rules, or other king of data profiling.

If you have implemented a Business Rules Engine as described above, you can easily use it to define and store your formatting and cleansing rules.

14.4 Master Data Management Engine

There is a special kind of data that we have to take care inside an EDWH. These data are called Master Data.

Master Data Management (MDM) comprises a set of processes, governance, policies, standards and tools that consistently defines and manages the master data (i.e. non-transactional data entities) of an organization (which may include reference data).

(Wikipedia, The Free Encyclopedia)

The usage is to manage the Enterprise Master Data outside of your Corporates Systems. In means that these Master Data should not be managed in your sources systems, neither in your EDWH.

We will discuss the concept of Master Data Management in another chapter, but here I would like to say that it is important to be aware that in an MDM system, some rules have to be applied to the data, and our role, as EDWH architect, is to be sure to be able to apply the same centrally defined rule to our data.

Let's take again the example of our retail company.

This retail company has a clear definition of what a consumer represents. It could be something like: "If a consumer has the same account number and the same email address as another consumer, we can merge these two consumers into a single one".

This definition is typically an MDM definition and should be considered as another Corporate Business Rule and exposed to other systems as a service.

Why?

In our retail company, we can imagine the following scenario:

Someone goes to the Company E-Commerce site, and create a new consumer profile. He fill-in all the requested fields, and after clicking the "finish" button, he receive a message: "We found another consumer with the same Email address and account number, is it you? Or someone in your household? Do you want to merge the two profiles or keep it separated?"

Our consumer received this message because at the moment of the click, an MDM service was called.

In an EDWH world, it often happens that we have to integrate external data. In the case of our retail company, we could imagine that we would have to integrate a list of prospects, to manage an emailing campaign.

Before sending a promotional email to these prospects, it could be useful to detect if we have in these prospects some in the same household who are already consumers!

In this classical example, we see that it is crucial to manage these MDM rules as Business Rules.

14.5 Other Services

In addition to the Business Rues Engine and the MDM Engine, you can find a series of other services in the Service Layer.

Among the most important, I can mention the service in charge of the back-ups and the archiving, as well as the one taking care of the LUW scheduling and orchestration.

CHAPTER 15
Transactional Unit Of Work

15.1 Nothing New Under The Sun

Yes, an EDWH is also made of transactions!

Although we are used to rightly oppose the worlds of transactional and analytical, we must face the fact that building an EDWH, as any other construction of databases, goes through the development of transactions.

> ***Transactions*** *provide an "all-or-nothing" proposition, stating that each work-unit performed in a database must either complete in its entirety or have no effect whatsoever. Further, the system must isolate each transaction from other transactions, results must conform to existing constraints in the database, and transactions that complete successfully must get written to durable storage.*
>
> (Wikipedia, The Free Encyclopedia)

We saw in a previous chapter that your development framework should suggest the use of Logical Unit Of Work. But to insure that your EDWH is consistent, you have to pipe your LUW into transactions which respects the ACID principles.

15.2 ACIDity of a Transaction

Processing a transaction often requires a sequence of operations that is subject to failure for a number of reasons. For instance, the system may have no room left on its disk drives, or it may have used up its allocated CPU time.

ACID (Atomicity, Consistency, Isolation, Durability) *is a set of properties that guarantee that database transactions are processed reliably. In the context of databases, a single logical operation on the data is called a transaction.*

(Wikipedia, The Free Encyclopedia)

Atomicity requires that each transaction is "all or nothing": if one part of the transaction fails, the entire transaction fails, and the database state is left unchanged.

Consistency ensures that any transaction will bring the database from one valid state to another. Any data written to the database must be valid according to all defined rules.

Isolation ensures that the concurrent execution of transactions results in a system state that would be obtained if transactions were executed serially, i.e. one after the other.

Durability means that once a transaction has been committed, it will remain so, even in the event of power loss, crashes, or errors. In a relational database, for instance, once a group of SQL statements execute, the results need to be stored permanently.

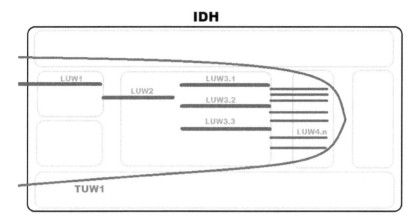

Figure 29 - LUW and TUW

15.3 LUW and TUW

We will see in the next two chapters, that the most important is to write correctly your Logical Unit Of Work. The creation of a Transactional Unit Of Work responding the ACID criteria will be manage by other services. The restartability and parallelism of your LUW will also be manage by an external service.

CHAPTER 16
Non Invasive Code

16.1 Small is great!

We have seen before that a Logical Unit of Work is the greatest piece of code an ETL Developer is authorized to write and that it should have a border to border scope.

We have also seen that it is our responsibility to populate the Metadata Layer in order to insure the Data Lineage and Impact Analysis.

How can we perform all these extra tasks, like counting the number of rows treated, tracking the starting and ending time of a transaction, creating the batch load ID, etc. without creating extra line of codes in our LUW?

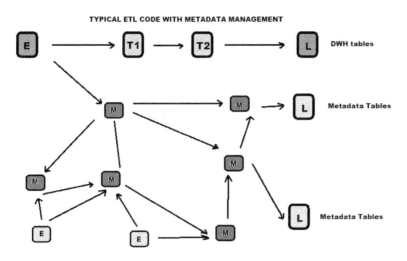

Figure 30 - Typical ETL Code

The first thing to keep in mind, is that the structure of our Metadata Layer is stable and maintained by us, so we know exactly where, when and what to write in it.

The second finding is that all these parasites tasks are repetitive and should be present in every single LUW.

As good programmer we are, we now that repetitive tasks should be externalized to a function or a procedure We could say to a service.

16.2 The Wrapper

If we decide to externalize the metadata tasks to a service, like we did for the business rules, we will consider these tasks as a transformation and they will be part of the T step of our ETL process. I personally do not think that this is a good idea!

The metadata tasks are not transformations and I consider it as parasite code. The idea here is to write Non Invasive Code. It means that all the code present in our LUWs is only to perform Extraction, Transformation (by calling a service) and Load tasks.

I propose you to write a special piece of code dedicated to the management of the metadata tasks.

For every LUW, you know that you have to create a load batch id, for tracking reasons; you have to write always the same information in your metadata layer like time stamps, number of treated rows, etc. You have also to collect information from external repositories, like processor and memory usage to track performance degradation for example.

Let's assume that you wrote piece of code doing all these tasks. I personally wrote mine in portable UNIX and I call it WRAPPER.

Your scheduler will have to launch your wrapper function, with the right parameters and this is it!

The syntax will look like this:

WRAPPER (LUW#, Technology);

My wrapper is able to launch a LUW written in T-SQL, ANSI SQL, PL-SQL, Informatica, BODS and DataStage and includes 12,000 lines of Unix code. But remember, you write the wrapper once, and then all your LUW are very simple and doing only what they are supposed to do!

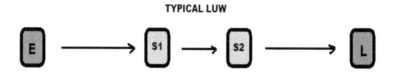

ORCHESTRATOR (WRAPPER (LUW#, TECHNO));

Figure 31 - Typical LUW

Do not forget to put your Wrapper code and the DDL of your metadata layer in a source code repository in order to manage the versioning of your code.

CHAPTER 17
Metadata Driven Automation

17.1 The End of the ETL Tools

It is now clear that ETL code is the heart of an EDWH. But, do we need an ETL tool to develop this code?

We have seen that our transactions are made of a series of Logical Unit Of Work, which by definition are very small and simple.

Why should we spend a lot of money to buy a complex tool to develop simple things?

And why should we be technology dependent?

My advice is to develop all your LUW in SQL, and if possible in pure ANSI SQL, so you are totally portable.

In addition, if you chose to use the Data Vault methodology to model the Core Data Warehouse Layer, you only have to develop three different patterns to load your data!

Indeed, you only have to find a generic way to load a Hub, another one to load the links and finally one to load the Satellites.

Once again, do you think you need an ETL tool to develop

three scripts?

17.2 Code Generation

For all the mentioned reasons, I have included in the IDH Framework, the concept of Metadata Driven Automation.

The idea is to describe what we want to develop, and let a code generator do the rest!

Let's take the example of our first layer, The Staging Layer.

We have seen before that the staging layer contains an image of the data of the sources system. Obviously the structure of the staging layer is the same as the structure of the source data, so the ETL we have to develop is very simple and is almost always a 1 to 1 transformation.

If you have to synchronize thousands of source tables in your staging layer, do you have to develop thousands of ETL scripts?

I do not think so!

The best practice would be to write a code generator able to develop for you these thousands of scripts.

We can do this way when developing very simple scripts, and obviously this is the case when populating the Staging Layer.

But, what about the other layers?

Traditionally the code to be developed to populate the Core Data Warehouse is the most complex, but if we adopt the Logical Unit Of Work concept and we use the Data Vault model it becomes very simple to develop these scripts, and most important, we can automatize the generation of these scripts, because the process to load a Data Vault Model is always the same, and each table can be loaded independently.

The process to load the Presentation Layer is more complex, especially if we use a dimensional model for this layer.

Complex, but not impossible to automatize!.

I will explain in a later chapter, how to deal with the load and the modeling of the presentation layer.

17.3 Metadata Driven

So now that we know that all the LUW can be generated,

how can we explain to the code generator what we want to develop?

Simply by describing what we want to do!

This is what I call Metadata Driven Automation.

And if your company is well organized and structured, you probably have some Business Analyst who have already described what you should develop. And the most common document use by ETL developer as an input from the Business Analyst is The Mapping Document, also called Source to Target Documents.

This document is normally very simple and consist most of the time of an Microsoft Excel document composed of three parts. One describing the source data, another one describing the transformation to apply to the data, and the last one describing the target format.

A typical mapping document should contain the following information's

- Mapping indicator(Values A:ADD, D:Delete,C:Change)
- Change description (Used to indicate mapping changes)
- Key Indication(Indicates whether the field is Primary

key or not)

- Source Table/File Name

- Source Field Name

- Source Field Data Type

- Source Field Length

- Source Field Description(The description will be used as a meta data for end user)

- Business Rule

- Target Table Name

- Target Field Name

- Target Data Type

- Target Field Length

- Comment

Mapping Indicator	Change Description on	Key Indicator	Source Table/File Name	Source Field name	Source Field Length	Source Data Type	Source Field Description	Business Rule	Target Table Name	Target Field Name	Target Data Type	Target Field Length	Comment
A		NA	Employee_info	Emp First Name	50	Text	Employee First Name	Direct Mapping	EMP_DIM	EMP_F_NME	Varchar	255	
A		NA	Employee_info	Emp Last Name	50	Text	Employee Last Name	Direct Mapping	EMP_DIM	EMP_L_NME	Varchar	255	
A		PK	Employee_info	EMP No	10	Number	Employee Number	Direct Mapping	EMP_DIM	EMP_NUM	Number	15	
A		NA	Employee_info	EMP Dep	50	Text	Employee Department	if Emp Dep="Sales" then load "S" Emp Dep="Packing" then load "P" Emp Dep="Transport" then load "T"	EMP_DIM	EMP_D_IND	Varchar	1	

Figure 32 - Mapping Document

As we have the mapping document at our disposal, let's use it to generate automatically our Logical Unit Of Work! And with a very good naming convention, the process becomes very simple!

In order to automate the generation of the loading code of the Data Vault components we ask ourselves these 3 simple questions:

- What distinguish a Hub from another?
- What distinguish a Link from another?
- What Distinguish a Sat from another?

The Answers are framed in the following figure and will constitute our Meta Data source for automation-

 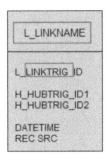 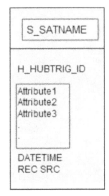

Figure 33 - Hub / Link / Satellite

Then,

with a good naming convention

a set of metadata tables

A vault Staging Step (to have 1 stage table to 1 or n vault table)

you can easily automate the loading of the data vault tables

17.4 Automation of the HUB Load

The principle is very simple and is the same for every single Hub!

To load a Hub, check if the Business Key already exists in this Hub. If it exists, you do nothing. I not, you insert it.

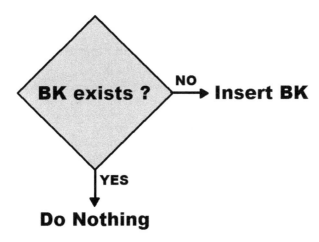

Figure 34 - Business Key exists in Hub?

To perform the Hub load, you only have to know the framed elements in the schema below.

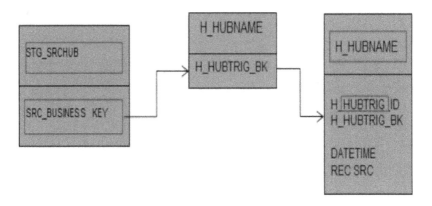

Figure 35 - Automated Hub Load

These elements constitute thus our metadata for the automation of the loading

> ### *To load a Hub,*
>
> *Take the business key from the staging table,*
>
> *Lookup the Hub on BK,*
>
> *Insert a new row if you don't find the BK, do nothing if it exists*

17.5 Automation of the LINK Load

To load a Link,

Take the business keys from the staging table,

Lookup the first Hub on BK and take the Hub ID,

Lookup the second Hub on BK and take the Hub ID (do that for all the Hubs of the Link)

Lookup the Link on Hub ID1 and Hub ID2...

Insert a new row if you don't find the IDs, do nothing if

they exists

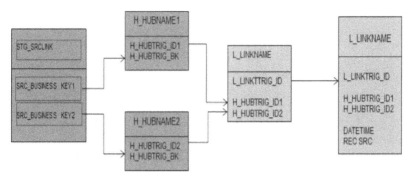

Figure 36 - Automated Link Load

17.6 Automation of the SAT Load

To load a Satellite on Hub or on Link,

Take the business key from the staging table,

Lookup the Hub on BK and take the Hub ID (do that for the other Hubs if Sat on Link)

Lookup the Link on Hub1 ID and Hub2 ID and take the link ID (for Sat on Link only)

Lockup the Sat on Sat ID

Insert a new row if you don't find the ID,

Update the row if the ID exist and one of the attribute is different

do nothing if all is equal

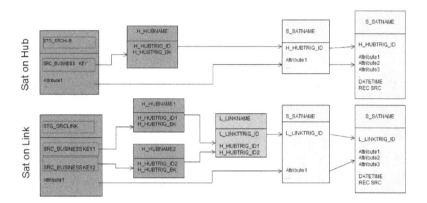

Figure 37 - Automated Sat Load

CHAPTER 18
The Message Oriented Layer

18.1 It's a HUB!

Do you remember the definition of the IDH™?

> *The **Integrated Data Hub**™ is a Hub of Integrated Data.*

Bu why a HUB?

Obviously our IDH is communicating with the external world in all the directions.

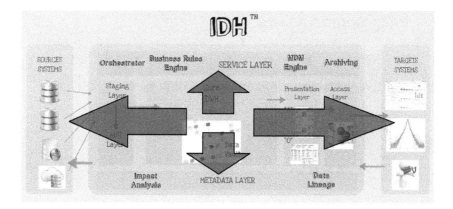

Figure 38 - It's a HUB!

The IDH™ has to communicate with the sources systems, by convention on the left, with the targets systems, on the right, with the metadata layer below and with the service layer on the top.

At the beginning of this book, I presented the IDH™ as the

perfect solution if you want to be less impacted by the external environment. We developed some concepts like the implementation of Data Vault to achieve this goal, but still we are dependent on changes in the sources systems. Not as much as before, but still to some degree.

To be more or I hope totally independent from the external world I have to introduce now a new concept. The Message Oriented Layer

18.2 Canonical Data

Before going further with the concept of Message Oriented Layer I have to talk about another important concept, The Data Canonicalization.

> The **Canonical Data Model** defines a common format to describe business entity within the enterprise wide organization

The data that are exchanged between systems have a defined format. If we take the example of a structured record, let's say an employee, you will probably find in any companies almost the same number and type of fields.

In some industries, some standards have appeared and if you do not want to define your own structure for your data, you can by a predefined one that will suit your needs.

It is obvious that if you have two different systems managing employee data, you will most probably have two different proprietary data structures. But imagine that you have a generic one defined by your enterprise, or even better, a generic one common to all your providers and your industry players. The exchange of data could be really tremendously eased.

This is already the case for some structure of data. Let's take the example of an MP3 file. The file will come with a set of predefined tags. It is not mandatory to fill in every single tag, but you are sure, that another system will be able to understand the file and to show correctly the content of these tags.

Believe me or not, we can use the same concept to exchange data between systems.

And, as already said, some industries has already published some standards, and you can easily buy a Canonical Model for retail, banking or pharmaceutical companies for example.

The last time I have implemented the IDH concepts we hired a Data Architect and he produced quite quickly an Enterprise Data Model.

18.3 XML Representation

An easy way to represent a canonical data it using an XML format. The XML format allows you to describe perfectly the structure of data and even to put in place a hierarchical dimension to your data.

```
<xsd:schema xmlns:xsd="http://www.w3.org/2001/XMLSchema">
 <xsd:element name="Customer" type="CustomerType"/>
  <xsd:complexType name="CustomerType">
   <xsd:sequence>
    <xsd:element name="NAME" type="xsd:string"/>
    <xsd:element name="EMAIL" type="xsd:string"/>
    <xsd:element name="ADDRESS" type="xsd:string"/>
    <xsd:element name="PHONE" type="phoneType"/>
    <xsd:element name="DESCRIPTION" type="contentType"/>
   </xsd:sequence>
  </xsd:complexType>
  <xsd:complexType name="ContentType" mixed="true">
   <xsd:sequence>
    <xsd:any minOccurs="0" maxOccurs="unbounded" processContents="skip"/>
   </xsd:sequence>
  </xsd:complexType>
  <xsd:simpleType name="phoneType">
   <xsd:restriction base="xsd:string">
    <xsd:pattern value="\(\d{3}\)\d{3}-\d{4}"/>
   </xsd:restriction>
  </xsd:simpleType>
</xsd:schema>
```

Figure 39 - XML Example

If your enterprise is mature enough to implement all the concepts of the IDH™, it probably already implemented a Messaging System for the real time communication between operational systems. This is often called an Enterprise Bus or a Service Oriented Architecture (SOA).

> *The purpose of **SOA** is to allow easy cooperation of a large number of computers that are connected over a network. Every computer can run an arbitrary number of programs - called services in this context - that are built in a way that they can exchange information with any other service within the reach of the network without human interaction and without the need to make changes to the underlying program itself.*
>
> (Wikipedia, The Free Encyclopedia)

If it is the case, I advise you to go to talk with your enterprise architecture, because he probably has already a canonical data model and all the knowledge to help you with these concepts.

18.4 Messaging

Now that the concept of canonical data is clear for everybody, let's go a step further.

Imagine that all your operational systems are able to read and understand your canonical data! Guess what? if you use standard industry software and an ERP it is probably the case. Indeed, Oracle, IBM, Microsoft, SAP etc. agreed on some standards for data interchanges.

And most probably these standards softwares are able to

understand simple message oriented commands like PUT and GET...

The concept of Message Oriented Layer in the IDH™ is eventually very simple. It consists in developing a Canonical Model and to use the enterprise Bus to get the needed data from the source systems and to write the data to the target systems.

Instead of requesting the EDWH to know exactly the structure of each single source table of every source system, and to know and master the best Change Data Capture method to receive only the desired data, imagine this dialog between the IDH and the source systems:

- **IDH**: Message to all listening systems dealing with customers: "I need all the customers' information that have been created or modified since last Monday. Give it to me in the enterprise canonical format please..."
- **ERP1**: Copy that! Sending ...
- **E-Commerce**: Copy that! Sending...
- **ERP2**: Copy That! Sending...
- **IDH:** Thank you all ! Talk to you soon!

Science fiction? No! Reality! Believe me, it works!

If another source system is coming to your environment, or one is decommissioned, there is no impact at all on your EDWH

If the structure of the data in one of your source systems changes there is no impact at all to your EDW.

We wanted to design a EDWH less impacted by the external world? It seems that the mission is accomplished...

CHAPTER 19
Leaf Schema™

19.1 A Star is Dead

I started this book by bumptiously saying that the Data Warehousing fathers stopped their thoughts too early, and now I will not less bumptiously say that I invented a new concept that will replace definitely the star schemas…

Of course I am not serious! I will only try here to explain that there is better model to host your presentation layer than a traditional Star Schema.

But let's start with some reminders.

19.2 Dimensional Modeling

I have already extensively covered the concepts of dimensional modeling in chapter 8. And remember, a Star Schema is made of a central Table containing the facts and surrounding table called Dimension.

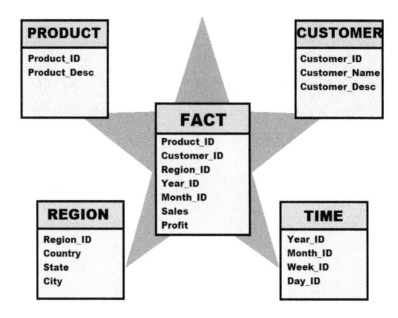

Figure 40 -Star Schema

Loading a Star Schema is not very difficult, but a certain sequence must be followed.

And obviously, there is a big difference in the structure of the stars schemas and the Data Vault Model.

How can we apply all the concepts of LUW, MetaData Driven Automation, etc. to go from one structure to the other?

Some tools have been developed to help you realize these transformations. Take a look to tools like Quipu and WhereScape for example.

But one of our challenges was to be technology independent. It would be very sad to abandon this rule so close to the goal.

19.3 A Leaf Is Born

Remember the Data Vault Modeling Concepts... Only three types of tables: Hubs, Links and Satellites... Hubs and links containing only the keys. The satellites are split by rate of change.

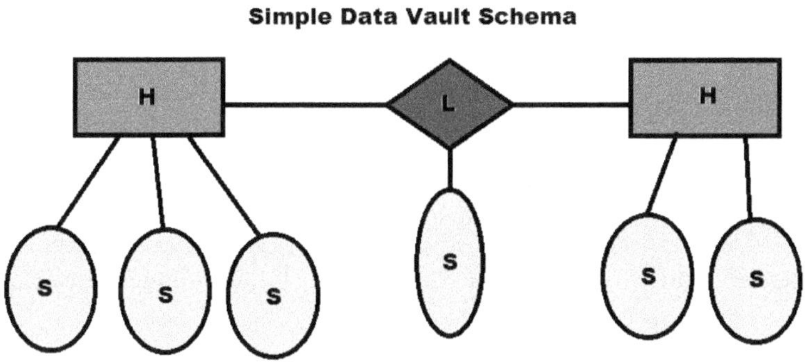

Simple Data Vault Schema

Figure 41 - Simple Data Vault Schema

Let's take a look to a very simple example: The relation between a customer and a product.

The Customer could look to something like this:

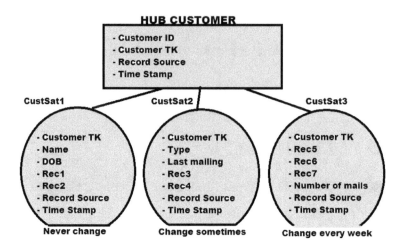

And if we decided to change a little the way we designed our satellites in our Business Data Vault Layer?

This is what I propose:

Let's put all the information destined to be part of a future dimension in dedicated satellites, and let's create a special satellite with the measures destined to go to a fact table.

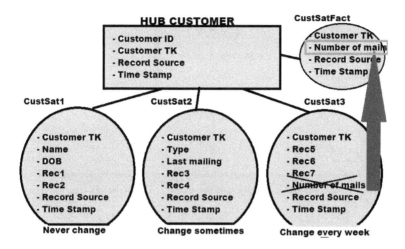

Figure 42 - Satellite with Facts

Now that we have all the future facts in separates satellites. Imagine the same process for the Products Satellites…

And here is the new concept: try to imagine a dimension made of small dimensions, with the same key.

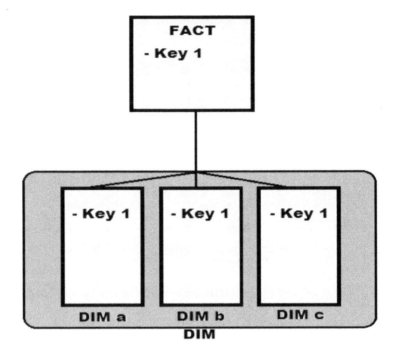

Figure 43 - Leaf

And yes, it is working!

Your final Data Mart will be a collection of Leafs as shown in the figure below.

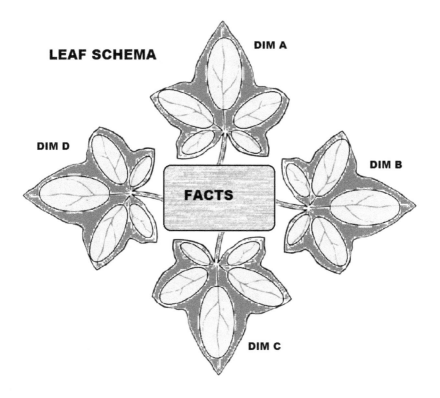

Figure 44 - Leaf Schema

Now we can see that the process to transform satellites into Leafs and Hub and dedicated satellites into Facts is very simple and most important it is automatable.

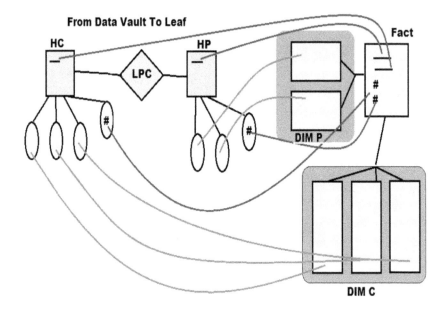

Figure 45 - Data Vault To Leaf

19.4 Virtualization

If you are looking for performance, you will probably start to think about hosting your presentation layer on an In Memory appliance.

Most of Business Intelligence providers are offering solutions to put your Data Mart in memory and to use virtualization techniques in order to gain in development time and performance.

A computer **appliance** *is generally a separate and discrete hardware device with integrated software (firmware), specifically designed to provide a specific computing resource. These devices became known as "appliances" because of their similarity to home appliances, which are generally "closed and sealed" – not serviceable by the owner. The hardware and software are pre-integrated and pre-configured before delivery to customer, to provide a "turn-key" solution to a particular problem. Unlike general purpose computers, appliances are generally not designed to allow the customers to change the software (including the underlying operating system), or to flexibly reconfigure the hardware.*

(Wikipedia, The Free Encyclopedia)

SAP Hana, Oracle Exadata, IBM Netezza are among the most important players in this domain.

With the Leaf Schema concept, you can imagine to use a view on your Data Vault Model to build virtual Data Marts. It is up to you to decide if you prefer to have a physical Data Mart or a virtual one.

In computing, a **data warehouse appliance** *is a marketing term for an integrated set of servers, storage, operating system(s), DBMS and software specifically pre-installed and pre-optimized for data warehousing (DW). Alternatively, the term can also apply to similar software-only systems promoted as easy to install on specific* *recommended hardware configurations or preconfigured as a complete system*

(Wikipedia, The Free Encyclopedia)

CHAPTER 20
A Working Example

20.1 Yes It Works!

As already mentioned, I successfully implemented the IDH concepts in different companies.

Each time I had to convince my teams, my management and the enterprise architects.

The best way to convince technical people is often by doing a simple proof of concept. And to explain the different concepts of the IDH™, I always use a sample database that everybody can understand.

20.2 Operational Schema

The schema is for Classic Models, a retailer of scale models of classic cars. The database contains typical business data such as customers, orders, order line items, products and so on.

The database consists of five tables:

- Customers
- Orders: Orders placed by customers
- Order Details: Line items within an order.
- Products: The list of scale model cars
- Product Lines: The list of product line classification

I found this sample database and the data to populate it on the elcipse.org website. The sample database is open source; you are free to use it for your own. The sample database is provided under the terms Eclipse.org Software User Agreement.

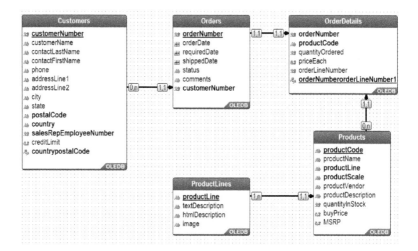

Figure 46 - OLTP Sample DB

I am convinced that everybody in your company can understand these sample data.

See below an extract of the Customers Data

customer-Number	customerName	contactLast-Name	contactFirst-Name	phone	addressLine1	addressLine2	city	state	postalCode	country	salesRepEmployee-Number	creditLimit
103	Atelier graphique	Schmitt	Carine	40.32.2555	54, rue Royale	NULL	Nantes	NULL	44000	France	1370	21000,00
112	Signal Gift Stores	King	Jean	7025551838	8489 Strong St.	NULL	Las Vegas	NV	83030	USA	1166	71800,00
114	Australian Collectors, Co.	Ferguson	Peter	03 9520 4555	636 St Kilda Road	Level 3	Melbourne	Victoria	3004	Australia	1611	117300,00
119	La Rochelle Gifts	Labrune	Janine	40.67.8555	67, rue des Cinquante O	NULL	Nantes	NULL	44000	France	1370	118200,00
121	Baane Mini Imports	Bergulfsen	Jonas	07-98 9555	Erling Skakkes gate 78	NULL	Stavern	NULL	4110	Norway	1504	81700,00
124	Mini Gifts Distributors Ltd.	Nelson	Susan	4155551450	5677 Strong St.	NULL	San Rafael	CA	97562	USA	1165	210500,00
125	Havel & Zbyszek Co	Piestrzeniewicz	Zbyszek	(26) 642-7555	ul. Filtrowa 68	NULL	Warszawa	NULL	01-012	Poland	0	0,00
128	Blauer See Auto, Co.	Keitel	Roland	+49 69 66 90 2555	Lyonerstr. 34	NULL	Frankfurt	NULL	60528	Germany	1504	59700,00
129	Mini Wheels Co.	Murphy	Julie	6505555787	5557 North Pendale Stre	NULL	San Francisco	CA	94217	USA	1165	64600,00
131	Land of Toys Inc.	Lee	Kwai	2125557818	897 Long Airport Avenue	NULL	NYC	NY	10022	USA	1323	114900,00
141	Euro+ Shopping Channel	Freyre	Diego	(91) 555 94 44	C/ Moralzarzal, 86	NULL	Madrid	NULL	28034	Spain	1370	227600,00
144	Volvo Model Replicas, Co	Berglund	Christina	0921-12 3555	Berguvsvägen 8	NULL	Luleå	NULL	S-958 22	Sweden	1504	53100,00
145	Danish Wholesale Imports	Petersen	Jytte	31 12 3555	Vinbæltet 34	NULL	Kobenhavn	NULL	1734	Denmark	1401	83400,00
146	Saveley & Henriot, Co.	Saveley	Mary	78.32.5555	2, rue du Commerce	NULL	Lyon	NULL	69004	France	1337	123900,00
148	Dragon Souveniers, Ltd.	Natividad	Eric	+65 221 7555	Bronz Sok.	Bronz Apt. 3/6 Tes	Singapore	NULL	079903	Singapore	1621	103800,00
151	Muscle Machine Inc	Young	Jeff	2125557413	4092 Furth Circle	Suite 400	NYC	NY	10022	USA	1286	138500,00
157	Diecast Classics Inc.	Leong	Kelvin	2155551555	7586 Pompton St.	NULL	Allentown	PA	70267	USA	1216	100600,00
161	Technics Stores Inc.	Hashimoto	Juri	6505556809	9408 Furth Circle	NULL	Burlingame	CA	94217	USA	1165	84600,00
166	Handji Gifts& Co	Victorino	Wendy	+65 224 1555	106 Linden Road Sando	2nd Floor	Singapore	NULL	069045	Singapore	1612	97900,00
167	Herkku Gifts	Oeztan	Veysel	+47 2267 3215	Brehmen St. 121	PR 334 Sentrum	Bergen	NULL	N 5804	Norway	1504	96800,00
168	American Souvenirs Inc	Franco	Keith	2035557845	149 Spinnaker Dr.	Suite 101	New Haven	CT	97823	USA	1286	0,00
169	Porto Imports Co.	de Castro	Isabel	(1) 356-5555	Estrada da saúde n. 58	NULL	Lisboa	NULL	1756	Portugal	0	0,00
171	Daedalus Designs Imports	Rancé	Martine	20.16.1555	184, chaussée de Tourn	NULL	Lille	NULL	59000	France	1370	82900,00
172	La Corne D'abondance, Co.	Bertrand	Marie	(1) 42.34.2555	265, boulevard Charonn	NULL	Paris	NULL	75012	France	1337	84300,00
173	Cambridge Collectables Co.	Tseng	Jerry	6175555555	4658 Baden Av.	NULL	Cambridge	MA	51247	USA	1188	43400,00
175	Gift Depot Inc.	King	Julie	2035552570	25593 South Bay Ln.	NULL	Bridgewater	CT	97562	USA	1323	84300,00
177	Osaka Souveniers Co.	Kentary	Mory	+81 06 6342 5555	1-6-20 Dojima	NULL	Kita-ku	Osaka	530-0003	Japan	1621	81200,00
181	Vitachrome Inc.	Frick	Michael	2125551500	2678 Kingston Rd.	Suite 101	NYC	NY	10022	USA	1286	76400,00
186	Toys of Finland, Co.	Karttunen	Matti	90-224 8555	Keskuskatu 45	NULL	Helsinki	NULL	21240	Finland	1501	96500,00
187	AV Stores, Co.	Ashworth	Rachel	(171) 555-1555	Fauntleroy Circus	NULL	Manchester	NULL	EC2 5NT	UK	1501	136800,00

Figure 47 - OLTP Customers Sample Data

And an extract of the Products and ProductLines data:

product-Code	productName	productLine	Product Scale	productVendor	productDescription	QuantityIn Stock	buy-Price	MSRP
S10_1678	1969 Harley Davidson Ultimate	Motorcycles	1:10	Min Lin Diecast	This replica features working kickstand, front suspension, gear-shift lever, footbrake lever, drive chain, wheels and steering. All parts are particularly delicate due to their precise scale and require special care and attention.	7933	48,81	95,70
S10_1949	1952 Alpine Renault 1300	Classic Cars	1:10	Classic Metal Creations	Turnable front wheels; steering function; detailed interior; detailed engine; opening hood; opening trunk; opening doors; and detailed chassis.	7305	98,58	214,30
S10_2016	1996 Moto Guzzi 1100i	Motorcycles	1:10	Highway 66 Mini Classics	Official Moto Guzzi logos and insignias, saddle bags located on side of motorcycle, detailed engine, working steering, working suspension, two leather seats, luggage rack, dual exhaust pipes, small saddle bag located on handle bars, two-tone paint with chrome accents, superior die-cast detail , rotating wheels , working kick stand, diecast metal with plastic parts and baked enamel finish.	6625	68,99	118,94
S10_4698	2003 Harley-Davidson Eagle D	Motorcycles	1:10	Red Start Diecast	Model features, official Harley Davidson logos and insignias, detachable rear wheelie bar, heavy diecast metal with resin parts, authentic multi-color tampo-printed graphics, separate engine drive belts, free-turning front fork, rotating tires and rear racing slick, certificate of authenticity, detailed engine, display stand , precision diecast replica, baked enamel finish, 1:10 scale model, removable fender, seat and tank cover piece for displaying the superior detail of the v-twin engine	5582	91,02	193,66
S10_4757	1972 Alfa Romeo GTA	Classic Cars	1:10	Motor City Art Classics	Features include: Turnable front wheels; steering function; detailed interior; detailed engine; opening hood; opening trunk; opening doors; and detailed chassis.	3252	85,68	136,00
S10_4962	1962 LanciaA Delta 16V	Classic Cars	1:10	Second Gear Diecast	Features include: Turnable front wheels; steering function; detailed interior; detailed engine; opening hood; opening trunk; opening doors; and detailed chassis.	6791	103,42	147,74
S12_1099	1968 Ford Mustang	Classic Cars	1:12	Autoart Studio Design	Hood, doors and trunk all open to reveal highly detailed interior features. Steering wheel actually turns the front wheels. Color dark green.	68	95,34	194,57
S12_1108	2001 Ferrari Enzo	Classic Cars	1:12	Second Gear Diecast	Turnable front wheels; steering function; detailed interior; detailed engine; opening hood; opening trunk; opening doors; and detailed chassis.	3619	95,59	207,80
S12_1666	1958 Setra Bus	Trucks and Buse	1:12	Welly Diecast Productions	Model features 30 windows, skylights & glare resistant glass, working steering system, original logos	1579	77,90	136,67
S12_2823	2002 Suzuki XREO	Motorcycles	1:12	Unimax Art Galleries	Official logos and insignias, saddle bags located on side of motorcycle, detailed engine, working steering, working suspension, two leather seats, luggage rack, dual exhaust pipes, small saddle bag located on handle bars, two-tone paint with chrome accents, superior die-cast detail , rotating wheels , working kick stand, diecast metal with plastic parts and baked enamel finish.	9997	66,27	150,62
S12_3148	1969 Corvair Monza	Classic Cars	1:18	Welly Diecast Productions	1:18 scale die-cast about 10" long doors open, hood opens, trunk opens and wheels roll	6906	89,14	151,08
S12_3380	1968 Dodge Charger	Classic Cars	1:12	Welly Diecast Productions	1:12 scale model of a 1968 Dodge Charger. Hood, doors and trunk all open to reveal highly detailed interior features. Steering wheel actually turns the front wheels. Color black	9123	75,16	117,44
S12_3891	1969 Ford Falcon	Classic Cars	1:12	Second Gear Diecast	Turnable front wheels; steering function; detailed interior; detailed engine; opening hood; opening trunk; opening doors; and detailed chassis.	1049	83,05	173,02
S12_3990	1970 Plymouth Hemi Cuda	Classic Cars	1:12	Studio M Art Models	Very detailed 1970 Plymouth Cuda model in 1:12 scale. The Cuda is generally accepted as one of the fastest original muscle cars from the 1970s. This model is a reproduction of one of the orginal 652 cars built in 1970. Red color.	5663	31,92	79,80
S12_4473	1957 Chevy Pickup	Trucks and Buse	1:12	Exoto Designs	1:12 scale die-cast about 20" long Hood opens, Rubber wheels	6125	55,70	118,50
S12_4675	1969 Dodge Charger	Classic Cars	1:12	Welly Diecast Productions	Detailed model of the 1969 Dodge Charger. This model includes finely detailed interior and exterior features. Painted in red and white.	7323	58,73	115,16
S18_1097	1940 Ford Pickup Truck	Trucks and Buse	1:18	Studio M Art Models	This model features soft rubber tires, working steering, rubber mud guards, authentic Ford logos, detailed undercarriage, opening doors and hood, removable split rear gate, full size spare mounted in bed, detailed interior with opening glove box	2613	58,33	116,67
S18_1129	1993 Mazda RX-7	Classic Cars	1:18	Highway 66 Mini Classics	This model features, opening hood, opening doors, detailed engine, rear spoiler, opening trunk, working steering, tinted windows, baked enamel finish. Color red.	3975	83,51	141,54

Figure 48 - OLTP Products Sample Data

productLine	textDescription	htmlDescription	image
Classic Cars	Attention car enthusiasts: Make your wildest car ownership dreams come true. Whether you are looking for classic muscle cars, dream sports cars or movie-inspired miniatures, you will find great choices in this category. These replicas feature superb attention to detail and craftsmanship and offer features such as working steering system, opening forward compartment, opening rear trunk with removable spare wheel, 4-wheel independent spring suspension, and so on. The models range in size from 1:10 to 1:24 scale and include numerous limited edition and several out-of-production vehicles. All models include a certificate of authenticity from their manufacturers and come fully assembled and ready for display in the home or office.	<html> <h4><font face="Verdana">Classic Cars</font></h4> <p><span style="font-family: Times New Roman">Attention car enthusiasts: Make your wildest car ownership dreams come true. Whether you are looking for <i><b>classic muscle cars</b></i>, <i><b>dream sports cars</b></i> or <i><b>movie-inspired miniatures</b></i>, </span> <font face="Times New Roman">from the early</font> <b><font face="Arial" size="2">1940s</font></b> <font face="Times New Roman">through the</font> <b> <font face="Arial" size="2">1980s</font></b> <span style="font-family: Times New Roman">you will find great choices in this [illegible]	
Motorcycles	Our motorcycles are state of the art replicas of classic as well as contemporary motorcycle legends such as Harley Davidson, Ducati and Vespa. Models contain stunning details such as official logos, rotating wheels, working kickstand, front suspension, gear-shift lever, footbrake lever, and drive chain. Materials used include diecast and plastic. The models range in size from 1:10 to 1:50 scale and include numerous limited edition and several out-of-production vehicles. All models come fully assembled and ready for display in the home or office. Most include a certificate of authenticity.	<html> <h4><font face="Verdana">Motorcycles</font></h4> <p><span style="font-family: Times New Roman; color: black">Our motorcycles are state of the art replicas of classic as well as contemporary motorcycle legends such as <i><b>Harley Davidson</b></i>, <i><b>Ducati</b></i> and <i><b>Vespa</b></i>. </span><span style="font-family: Times New Roman">Models contain stunning details such as official logos, rotating wheels, working kickstand, front suspension, gear-shift lever, footbrake lever, and drive chain. <span style="color:#111111">M</span>aterials used include <i><b>diecast</b></i> and <i><b>plastic</b></i>. <span style="color: black">The models range in size from [illegible]	
Planes	Unique, diecast airplane and helicopter replicas suitable for collections, as well as home, office or classroom decorations. Models contain stunning details such as official logos and insignias, rotating jet engines and propellers, retractable wheels, and so on. Most come fully assembled and with a certificate of authenticity from their manufacturers.	<html> <h4><font face="Verdana">Planes</font></h4> <p><span style="font-family: Times New Roman">Unique, <i><b>diecast</b></i> airplane and helicopter replicas suitable for collections, as well as home, office or classroom decorations. Models contain stunning details such as official logos and insignias, rotating jet engines and propellers, retractable wheels, and so on. Most come <span style="color: black"><i><b>fully assembled</b></i> and with a <i><b>certificate of authenticity</b></i> from their manufacturers.</span></span><span style="font-size: 10.0pt; font-family: Arial"> </span></p>	

Figure 49 - OLTP ProductLines Sample Data

And last but not least the Orders and Order Details data

orderNumber	orderDate	requiredDate	shippedDate	status	comments	customerNumber
10100	06/01/2003	13/01/2003	10/01/2003	Shipped	NULL	363
10101	09/01/2003	18/01/2003	11/01/2003	Shipped	Check on availability	128
10102	10/01/2003	18/01/2003	14/01/2003	Shipped	NULL	181
10103	29/01/2003	07/02/2003	02/02/2003	Shipped	NULL	121
10104	31/01/2003	09/02/2003	01/02/2003	Shipped	NULL	141
10105	11/02/2003	21/02/2003	12/02/2003	Shipped	NULL	145
10106	17/02/2003	24/02/2003	21/02/2003	Shipped	NULL	278
10107	24/02/2003	03/03/2003	26/02/2003	Shipped	Difficult to negotiate with customer. We need more marketing materials	131
10108	03/03/2003	12/03/2003	08/03/2003	Shipped	NULL	385
10109	10/03/2003	19/03/2003	11/03/2003	Shipped	Customer requested that FedEx Ground is used for this shipping	486
10110	18/03/2003	24/03/2003	20/03/2003	Shipped	NULL	187
10111	25/03/2003	31/03/2003	30/03/2003	Shipped	NULL	129
10112	24/03/2003	03/04/2003	29/03/2003	Shipped	Customer requested that ad materials (such as posters, pamphlets) be included in the shipment	144
10113	26/03/2003	02/04/2003	27/03/2003	Shipped	NULL	124
10114	01/04/2003	07/04/2003	02/04/2003	Shipped	NULL	172
10115	04/04/2003	12/04/2003	07/04/2003	Shipped	NULL	424
10116	11/04/2003	19/04/2003	13/04/2003	Shipped	NULL	381
10117	16/04/2003	24/04/2003	17/04/2003	Shipped	NULL	148
10118	21/04/2003	29/04/2003	26/04/2003	Shipped	Customer has worked with some of our vendors in the past and is aware of their MSRP	216
10119	28/04/2003	05/05/2003	02/05/2003	Shipped	NULL	382
10120	29/04/2003	08/05/2003	01/05/2003	Shipped	NULL	114
10121	07/05/2003	13/05/2003	13/05/2003	Shipped	NULL	353
10122	08/05/2003	18/05/2003	13/05/2003	Shipped	NULL	350
10123	20/05/2003	29/05/2003	22/05/2003	Shipped	NULL	103
10124	21/05/2003	29/05/2003	25/05/2003	Shipped	Customer very concerned about the exact color of the models. There is high risk that he may dispute the order because there is a slight color mismatch	112
10125	21/05/2003	27/05/2003	24/05/2003	Shipped	NULL	114
10126	28/05/2003	07/06/2003	02/06/2003	Shipped	NULL	458
10127	03/06/2003	09/06/2003	06/06/2003	Shipped	Customer requested special shippment. The instructions were passed along to the warehouse	151
10128	06/06/2003	12/06/2003	11/06/2003	Shipped	NULL	141
10129	12/06/2003	18/06/2003	14/06/2003	Shipped	NULL	324

Figure 50 - OLTP Orders Sample Data

orderNumber	productCode	quantityOrdered	priceEach	orderLineNumber	orderNumberorderLineNumber1
10100	S24_3969	49	35.290000	1	10100,1
10100	S18_2248	50	55.090000	2	10100,2
10100	S10_2016	30	136.000000	3	10100,3
10100	S18_4409	22	75.460000	4	10100,4
10101	S18_2795	26	167.060000	1	10101,1
10101	S24_2022	46	44.350000	2	10101,2
10101	S24_1937	45	32.530000	3	10101,3
10101	S18_2325	25	108.060000	4	10101,4
10102	S18_1367	41	43.130000	1	10102,1
10102	S18_1342	39	95.550000	2	10102,2
10103	S24_2300	36	107.340000	1	10103,1
10103	S18_2432	22	58.340000	2	10103,2
10103	S32_1268	31	92.460000	3	10103,3
10103	S10_4962	42	119.670000	4	10103,4
10103	S18_4600	36	98.070000	5	10103,5
10103	S700_2824	42	94.070000	6	10103,6
10103	S32_3522	45	63.350000	7	10103,7
10103	S12_1666	27	121.640000	8	10103,8
10103	S18_4668	41	40.750000	9	10103,9
10103	S18_1097	35	94.500000	10	10103,10
10103	S10_1949	26	214.300000	11	10103,11
10103	S18_2949	27	92.190000	12	10103,12
10103	S18_3136	25	86.920000	13	10103,13
10103	S18_2957	35	61.840000	14	10103,14
10103	S24_4258	25	88.620000	15	10103,15
10103	S18_3320	46	86.310000	16	10103,16
10104	S12_3148	34	131.440000	1	10104,1
10104	S50_1514	32	53.310000	2	10104,2
10104	S18_4027	38	119.200000	3	10104,3
10104	S32_3207	49	56.550000	4	10104,4
10104	S24_4048	26	106.450000	5	10104,5
10104	S24_1444	35	52.020000	6	10104,6
10104	S50_1392	33	114.590000	7	10104,7
10104	S18_2238	24	135.900000	8	10104,8
10104	S12_4473	41	111.390000	9	10104,9
10104	S24_2840	44	30.410000	10	10104,10
10104	S32_2509	35	51.950000	11	10104,11
10104	S18_2319	29	122.730000	12	10104,12
10104	S18_3232	23	165.950000	13	10104,13

Figure 51 - OLTP Order Details Sample Data

Note that I have created in the Staging version of the Order Details table; a composite key made of the Product Key and the

Order Line Number: Doing this, I will be able to create a unique key which will become a Business Key in my Data Vault model.

20.3 Data Vault Schema

Let's take a look to a possible Data Vault model for our Classic Model Company.

It is obvious that the Customer is a business entity represented by a Business Key which is the Customer Number.

We will thus have a Customer Hub.

As some attributes are almost never changing and other are most likely changing often, I will create two Satellites attached to the Customer Hub.

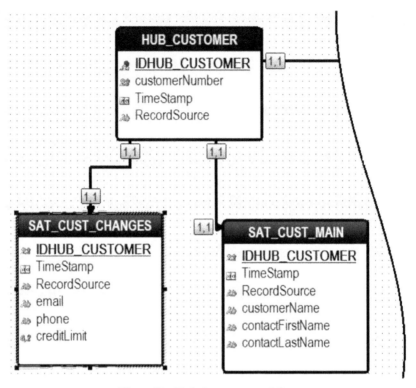

Figure 52 - Hub Customers and Sats

We will have the same approach to model the Orders Hub, and then we link these two Hubs together.

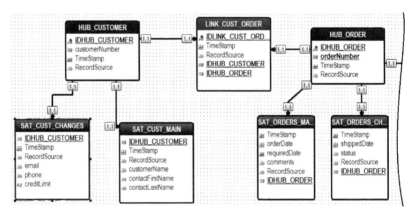

Figure 53 - Links between Orders and Customers

The trickiest part comes now!

Do you think that OrderDetails is a Hub or a Link?

Remember; I chose to create a Unique Business Key in my Order Details staging Table, because I always chose to model it as a Hub.

If you are not convinced, I advise you to read a book on Data Vault Modeling: I recommend you the excellent book of my friend Hans Hultgren: "Modeling The Agile Data Warehouse With Data Vault" or to register to one of his master classes on Genesee Academy!

And of course, you will create a Product Hub.

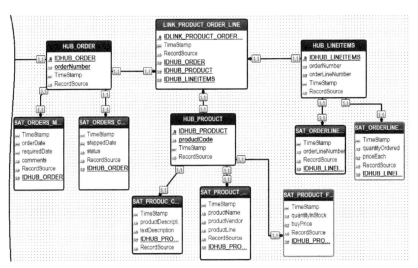

Figure 54 - Link between Orders Products and Lines

Note that I have created two special satellites containing measures. One attached to the Product Hub and one attached to the LinesItems Hub.

These two special satellites are destined to become facts in our Data Mart layer.

The final Data Vault model could look like the one presented in the next figure.

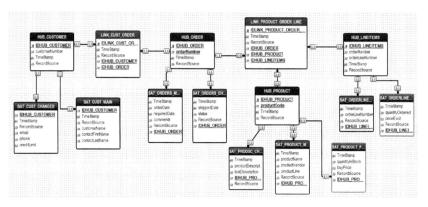

Figure 55 - A Customer / Orders Data Vault Model

20.4 Data Mart Schema

We know that the Data Vault model is not designed to be queried. We have thus now to design a dedicated model for our presentation layer.

If you opt for a Star Schema, your model could be similar to the following one:

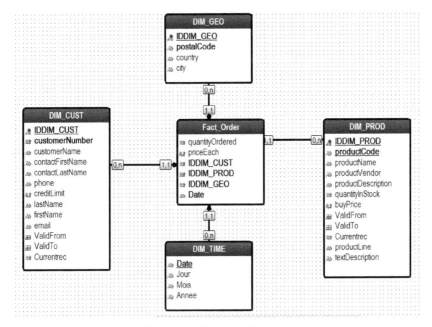

Figure 56 - Order Star Schema

Or you can opt, like I recommend for a Leaf Schema, and your transformation process to go From Data Vault to Data Mart will be reduced.

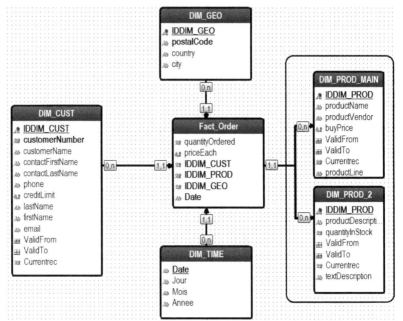

Figure 57 - Orders Leaf Schema

CHAPTER 21
Conclusions

21.1 A Never Ending Story

After more than 23 year of professional experience managing projects related to Data Management, I have seen the evolution of my discipline.

The importance of data for a modern company is still underestimated, but over the past few years I can see positives signs showing that top managers are now more and more convinced that they have to invest more in technologies and people able to transform the large amount data generated by their companies into a competitive advantage.

In some, but unfortunately still too few companies, a Chief Data Officer position has been created. This means that eventually there is someone able to talk about the importance of data at the board level. This is very encouraging!

As the importance of data grows, it is important to adopt the right methodologies and strategies to manage it. I have tried trough this book to give you a set of tools and tips to avoid the majority of traps an Enterprise Data Architect could face when deploying a central repository of Data.

Remember that the Integrated Data Hub™ is a proposed reference architecture and a set of best practices. It is up to you, depending of your challenges, your budget and the maturity of your company to decide to deploy it totally or to take only some components of it.

I have already deployed the IDH concepts in three different environments, and each time it was different. Each time I had to make adaptations as the concepts evolved. And for sure, it will continue to evolve to adapt to new challenges and technologies.

I hope this little contribution to the fascinating world of data and information was helpful to some of you.

Do not hesitate to contact me for more information and of course to share your successes.

About The Author

Dario Mangano is an executive with over 23 years of global IT management and consulting experience. In his current role as Head Of Knowledge Management of an international retail group, he manages the Business Intelligence, Enterprise Content Management and Global Data Services departments and drives the transformation of structured data, as well as unstructured and big data into information and knowledge. The motto of his department is indeed: "From Data, To Information, To Knowledge, To Actions!»

Dario is also an renowned international keynote speaker.

In addition, he is a certified Data Vault Modeler and the founder of the Swiss Network of Business Intelligence Professionals.

Figure 58 - 1st IDH Brainstorming

Table of Figures

Bibliography

From Wikipedia, the free encyclopedia. (n.d.). *Bank Of America*. Retrieved December 2012, from From Wikipedia, the free encyclopedia: http://en.wikipedia.org/wiki/Bank_of_america

From Wikipedia, the free encyclopedia. (n.d.). *Data Integration*. Retrieved December 2012, from From Wikipedia, the free encyclopedia: http://en.wikipedia.org/wiki/Data_integration

From Wikipedia, the free encyclopedia. (n.d.). *Data Vault Modeling*. Retrieved March 2013, from From Wikipedia, the free encyclopedia: http://en.wikipedia.org/wiki/Data_Vault_Modeling

From Wikipedia, the free encyclopedia. (n.d.). *Data Vault Modeling*. Retrieved March 2013, from From Wikipedia, the free encyclopedia: http://en.wikipedia.org/wiki/Data_Vault_Modeling

From Wikipedia, the free encyclopedia. (n.d.). *Mergers and acuisition*. Retrieved December 2012, from Wikipedia: http://en.wikipedia.org/wiki/Mergers_and_acquisitions

From Wikipedia, the free encyclopedia. (n.d.). *Natural Key*. Retrieved March 2013, from From Wikipedia, the free encyclopedia: http://en.wikipedia.org/wiki/Natural_key

From Wikipedia, the free encyclopedia. (n.d.). *Semantic Layer*. Retrieved June 2013, from Wikipedia: http://en.wikipedia.org/wiki/Semantic_layer

From Wikipedia, the free encyclopedia. (n.d.). *The DIKW Pyramid*. Retrieved December 2012, from From Wikipedia, the free encyclopedia: http://en.wikipedia.org/wiki/DIKW

From Wikipedia, the free encyclopedia. (n.d.). *The Operational Data Store*. Retrieved December 2012, from From Wikipedia, the free encyclopedia: http://en.wikipedia.org/wiki/Operational_data_store

Gartner. (n.d.). *Big Data IT Glossary*. Retrieved December 2012, from Gartner: http://www.gartner.com/it-glossary/big-data/

Hultgren, Hans. (2012, September). *Data Vault Modeling Guide*. Retrieved June 2013, from Hans Hultgren's Blog: http://hanshultgren.files.wordpress.com/2012/09/data-vault-modeling-guide.pdf

Hultgren, Hans. (2012, September). *Data Vault Modleing Guide*. Retrieved June 2013, from Hans Hultgren's Blog: http://hanshultgren.files.wordpress.com/2012/09/data-vault-modeling-guide.pdf

Hultgren, Hans. (2012). Hub Sequence ID. In H. Hultgren, *Modeling The Agile Data Warehouse With Data Vault* (p. 88). New Hamilton.

Hultgren, Hans. (2012). Satellite Sequence ID FK. In H. Hultgren, *Modeling The Agile Data Warehouse With Data Vault* (p. 117). New Hamilton.

Hultgren, Hans. (2012). The Link. In H. Hultgren, *Modeling The Agile Data Warehouse Using Data Vault* (p. 94). New Hamilton.

Imhoff, Claudia. (1999). *Information Management*. Retrieved March 2013, from http://www.information-management.com/issues/19991201/1667-1.html: http://www.information-management.com/issues/19991201/1667-1.html

Inmon, Bill. (2000, July 1). *Operational and Informational Reporting*. Retrieved June 2013, from Information Management: http://www.information-management.com/issues/20000701/2349-1.html

Janssen, Cory. (2012). *Third Normal Form (3NF)*. Retrieved March 2013, from Techopedia: http://www.techopedia.com/definition/22561/third-normal-form-3nf

Linstedt, Dan. (2004). *Data Vault Series 4 - Link Tables*. Retrieved March 2013, from The Data Administration Newsletter: http://www.tdan.com/view-articles/5172/

Linstedt, Dan. (2010). *How to Build an Effective Data Vault Model*. Retrieved March 2013, from How to Build an Effective Data Vault Model: http://danLinstedt.com

Michelle A. Poolet. (2007, December 18). *Data Warehousing: Slowly Changing Dimensions*. Retrieved January 2013, from SQLMAG: http://www.sqlmag.com/article/data-management/data-warehousing-slowly-changing-dimensions-97409

Michelle A. Poolet. (2007, October 25). *The Data Warehouse Bus Architecture*. Retrieved January 2013, from SQL MAG: http://www.sqlmag.com/article/data-management/the-data-warehouse-bus-architecture-96926

Poolet, Michelle A. (2007, October 25). *The Data Warehouse Bus Architecture*. Retrieved March 2013, from SQL Mag: http://www.sqlmag.com/article/data-management/the-data-warehouse-bus-architecture-96926

Ravo's Business Intelligence. (n.d.). *Ravo's Business Intelligence*. Retrieved December 2012, from Ravo's Business Intelligence: http://roelantvos.com/blog/?page_id=52

Ross, Margie. (2008). *Kimball Core Concepts*. Retrieved March 2013, from Kimball Group: http://www.kimballgroup.com/data-warehouse-and-business-intelligence-resources/kimball-core-concepts/

Rouse, Margaret. (2010, September). *Star Schema Definition*. Retrieved March 2013, from TechTarget: http://searchdatamanagement.techtarget.com/definition/star-schema

Rouse, Margaret. (2012, April). *What is OLAP Cube?* Retrieved June 2013, from SearchDataManagement: http://searchdatamanagement.techtarget.com/definition/OLAP-cube

Techopedia.com - The IT Education Site. (n.d.). *Data Lineage*. Retrieved June 2013, from Techopedia.com - The IT Education Site: http://www.techopedia.com/definition/28040/data-lineage

Wikipedia, The Free Encyclopedia. (n.d.). *ACID*. Retrieved August 2013, from Wikipedia, The Free Encyclopedia: http://en.wikipedia.org/wiki/ACID

Wikipedia, The Free Encyclopedia. (n.d.). *Computer Appliance*. Retrieved August 2013, from Wikipedia, The Free Encyclopedia: http://en.wikipedia.org/wiki/Computer_appliance

Wikipedia, The Free Encyclopedia. (n.d.). *Data warehouse appliance*. Retrieved August 2013, from Wikipedia, The Free Encyclopedia: http://en.wikipedia.org/wiki/Data_warehouse_appliance

Wikipedia, The Free Encyclopedia. (n.d.). *Database transaction*. Retrieved August 2013, from Wikipedia, The Free Encyclopedia: http://en.wikipedia.org/wiki/Database_transaction

Wikipedia, The Free Encyclopedia. (n.d.). *Drill Down*. Retrieved June 2013, from Wikipedia, The Free Encyclopedia: http://en.wikipedia.org/wiki/Drill_down

Wikipedia, The Free Encyclopedia. (n.d.). *Master data management*. Retrieved August 2013, from Wikipedia, The Free Encyclopedia: http://en.wikipedia.org/wiki/Master_data_management

Wikipedia, The Free Encyclopedia. (n.d.). *Metadata and data warehousing*. Retrieved June 2013, from Wikipedia, The Free Encyclopedia: https://en.wikipedia.org/wiki/Metadata

Wikipedia, The Free Encyclopedia. (n.d.). *Service-oriented architecture*. Retrieved August 2013, from Wikipedia, The Free Encyclopedia: http://en.wikipedia.org/wiki/Service-oriented_architecture